BIBLE WISDOM
FOR Newlyweds

COMPILED BY GARY WILDE

Christian Parenting
BOOKS

Christian Parenting Books is an imprint of
Chariot Family Publishing, a division of
David C. Cook Publishing Co., Elgin, Illinois 60120
David C. Cook Publishing Co., Weston, Ontario
Nova Distribution Ltd., Newton Abbot, England

Christian Parenting Today Magazine
P.O. Box 850, Sisters, OR 97759 (800) 238-2221

BIBLE WISDOM FOR NEWLYWEDS
© 1994 by Chariot Family Publishing

Cover design by Foster Design Associates
Interior design by Glass House Graphics
Compiled by Gary Wilde

First Printing, 1994 ISBN 0-78140-145-3
Printed in the United States of America
98 97 96 95 94 5 4 3 2 1

═══TABLE OF CONTENTS═══

Chapter 1

'Do I have the commitment to make this marriage work?'

I know Beverly and I will face our tough times in the years ahead," said Marty. "But if we can keep our spiritual lives strong and growing, we can face those trying times together, with the Lord's strength. Everything that happens in our marriage and family can be a witness to God's grace.

"It's comforting—and scary too—to know that I can't engineer everything in my life to my own satisfaction. I never could do that when I was single, and it's certain I won't be able to do it now that there are two of us. We'll both need to let God be in charge of the Happiness Department."

FOR MEMORY:

Consider it pure joy, my brothers, whenever you face trials of many kinds, because you know that the testing of your faith develops perseverance. Perseverance must finish its work so that you may be mature and complete, not lacking anything.

James 1:2-4

FOR SILENT REFLECTION:

- *How do I respond when I face obstacles, disappointments, or challenges?*

- *When have I shown a high degree of commitment in the past? How can that experience help me to understand commitment and perseverance in marriage?*

- *To what extent have I discussed with my spouse my concerns, fears, or hurts related to our relationship?*

- *What values will help us keep our commitment strong?*

It Takes Perseverance to Build a Marriage

Do you not know that in a race all the runners run, but only one gets the prize? Run in such a way as to get the prize. Everyone who competes in the games goes into strict training. They do it to get a crown that will not last; but we do it to get a crown that will last forever. Therefore I do not run like a man running aimlessly; I do not fight like a man beating the air. No, I beat my body and make it my slave so that after I have preached to others, I myself will not be disqualified for the prize.

I Corinthians 9:24-27

Therefore, since we are surrounded by such a great cloud of witnesses, let us throw off everything that hinders and the sin that so easily entangles, and let us run with perseverance the race marked out for us. Let us fix our eyes on Jesus, the author and perfecter of our faith, who for the joy set before him endured the cross, scorning its shame, and sat down at the right hand of the throne of God. Consider him who endured such opposition from sinful men, so that you will not grow weary and lose heart. In your struggle against sin, you have not yet resisted to the point of shedding your blood.

Hebrews 12:1-4

Let us not become weary in doing good, for at the proper time we will reap a harvest if we do not give up.

Galatians 6:9

"Anyone who does not carry his cross and follow me cannot be my disciple. Suppose one of you wants to build a tower. Will he not first sit down and estimate the cost to see if he has enough money to complete it? For if he lays the foundation and is not able to finish it, everyone who sees it will ridicule him, saying, 'This fellow began to build and was not able to finish.'

"Or suppose a king is about to go to war against another king. Will he not first sit down and consider whether he is able with ten thousand men to oppose the one coming against him with twenty thousand? If he is not able, he will send a delegation while the other is still a long way off and will ask for terms of peace. In the same way, any of you who does not give up everything he has cannot be my disciple.

"Salt is good, but if it loses its saltiness, how can it be made salty again? It is fit neither for the soil nor for the manure pile; it is thrown out. He who has ears to hear, let him hear."

Luke 14:27-35

Though the fig tree does not bud

and there are no grapes on the vines,
though the olive crop fails
and the fields produce no food,
though there are no sheep in the pen
and no cattle in the stalls,
yet I will rejoice in the LORD,
I will be joyful in God my Savior.
The Sovereign LORD is my strength;
he makes my feet like the feet of a deer,
he enables me to go on the heights.

Habakkuk 3:17-19

When You Feel Fearful in the Face of Marital Challenges

Be merciful to me, O LORD,
for I am in distress;
my eyes grow weak with sorrow,
my soul and my body with grief.
My life is consumed by anguish
and my years by groaning;
my strength fails because of my affliction,
and my bones grow weak.
Because of all my enemies,
I am the utter contempt of my neighbors;
I am a dread to my friends—
those who see me on the street flee from me.

I am forgotten by them as though I were dead;
I have become like broken pottery.
For I hear the slander of many;
there is terror on every side;
they conspire against me and plot to take my life.

Psalm 31:9-13

Be strong and courageous. Do not be afraid or terrified because of them, for the LORD your God goes
with you; he will never leave you nor forsake you.

Deuteronomy 31:6

Have I not commanded you? Be strong and courageous. Do not be terrified; do not be discouraged, for
the LORD your God will be with you wherever you
go.

Joshua 1:9

Though an army besiege me, my heart will not fear;
though war break out against me, even then will I be
confident.

Psalm 27:3

For God did not give us a spirit of timidity, but a
spirit of power, of love and of self-discipline.

II Timothy 1:7

There is no fear in love. But perfect love drives out

fear, because fear has to do with punishment. The one who fears is not made perfect in love.

I John 4:18

Renew Your Strength for Making Your Marriage Work

It is the Sovereign LORD who helps me.
Who is he that will condemn me?
They will all wear out like a garment;
the moths will eat them up.
Who among you fears the LORD
and obeys the word of his servant?
Let him who walks in the dark,
who has no light, trust in the name of the LORD
and rely on his God.

Isaiah 50:9, 10

Come to me, all you who are weary and burdened, and I will give you rest.

Matthew 11:28

"Blessed are those who mourn, for they will be comforted. Blessed are the meek, for they will inherit the earth. Blessed are those who hunger and thirst for righteousness, for they will be filled. Blessed are the merciful, for they will be shown mercy. Blessed are the pure in heart, for they will see God. Blessed are

17

the peacemakers, for they will be called sons of God. Blessed are those who are persecuted because of righteousness, for theirs is the kingdom of heaven. Blessed are you when people insult you, persecute you and falsely say all kinds of evil against you because of me. Rejoice and be glad, because great is your reward in heaven, for in the same way they persecuted the prophets who were before you."

Matthew 5:4-12

Therefore, strengthen your feeble arms and weak knees. "Make level paths for your feet," so that the lame may not be disabled, but rather healed. Make every effort to live in peace with all men and to be holy; without holiness no one will see the Lord. See to it that no one misses the grace of God and that no bitter root grows up to cause trouble and defile many.

Hebrews 12:12-15

Hold to Personal Values That Contribute to Being a Good Spouse

• *Looking to God for Leadership and Guidance*
I will instruct you and teach you in the way you should go;
I will counsel you and watch over you.

Psalm 32:8

Guide me in your truth and teach me,
for you are God my Savior,
and my hope is in you all day long.
Remember, O LORD, your great mercy and love,
for they are from of old.
Remember not the sins of my youth
and my rebellious ways; according to your love
remember me,
for you are good, O LORD.
Good and upright is the LORD;
therefore he instructs sinners in his ways.
He guides the humble in what is right
and teaches them his way.

Psalm 25:5-9

Teach me your way, O LORD;
lead me in a straight path because of my oppressors.

Psalm 27:11

For this God is our God for ever and ever;
he will be our guide even to the end.

Psalm 48:14

Trust in the LORD with all your heart
and lean not on your own understanding;
in all your ways acknowledge him,
and he will make your paths straight.

Proverbs 3:5, 6

19

I will lead the blind by ways they have not known,
along unfamiliar paths I will guide them;
I will turn the darkness into light before them
and make the rough places smooth.
These are the things I will do;
I will not forsake them.

Isaiah 42:16

For the LORD'S portion is his people, Jacob his allotted inheritance. In a desert land he found him, in a barren and howling waste. He shielded him and cared for him; he guarded him as the apple of his eye, like an eagle that stirs up its nest and hovers over its young, that spreads its wings to catch them and carries them on its pinions. The LORD alone led him; no foreign god was with him. He made him ride on the heights of the land and fed him with the fruit of the fields. He nourished him with honey from the rock, and with oil from the flinty crag, with curds and milk from herd and flock and with fattened lambs and goats, with choice rams of Bashan and the finest kernels of wheat. You drank the foaming blood of the grape.

Deuteronomy 32:9-14

• *Self-discipline and Trustworthiness*
Therefore, brothers, we have an obligation—but it is not to the sinful nature, to live according to it. For if

20

you live according to the sinful nature, you will die; but if by the Spirit you put to death the misdeeds of the body, you will live.

Romans 8:12, 13

Those who belong to Christ Jesus have crucified the sinful nature with its passions and desires.

Galatians 5:24

For the grace of God that brings salvation has appeared to all men. It teaches us to say "No" to ungodliness and worldly passions, and to live self-controlled, upright and godly lives in this present age.

Titus 2:11, 12

Consider it pure joy, my brothers, whenever you face trials of many kinds, because you know that the testing of your faith develops perseverance. Perseverance must finish its work so that you may be mature and complete, not lacking anything. Blessed is the man who perseveres under trial, because when he has stood the test, he will receive the crown of life that God has promised to those who love him.

James 1:2-4, 12

•*A Stong Base of Values*

Do not conform any longer to the pattern of this world, but be transformed by the renewing of your mind. Then you will be able to test and approve what God's will is—his good, pleasing and perfect will.

Romans 12:2

Since, then, you have been raised with Christ, set your hearts on things above, where Christ is seated at the right hand of God. Set your minds on things above, not on earthly things. For you died, and your life is now hidden with Christ in God. When Christ, who is your life, appears, then you also will appear with him in glory. Put to death, therefore, whatever belongs to your earthly nature: sexual immorality, impurity, lust, evil desires and greed, which is idolatry. Because of these, the wrath of God is coming.

Colossians 3:1-6

Do not love the world or anything in the world. If anyone loves the world, the love of the Father is not in him. For everything in the world—the cravings of sinful man, the lust of his eyes and the boasting of what he has and does—comes not from the Father but from the world. The world and its desires pass away, but the man who does the will of God lives forever.

I John 2:15-17

For everyone born of God overcomes the world. This is the victory that has overcome the world, even our faith. Who is it that overcomes the world? Only he who believes that Jesus is the Son of God.

I John 5:4, 5

•*Courage*

Then Moses summoned Joshua and said to him in the presence of all Israel, "Be strong and courageous, for you must go with this people into the land that the LORD swore to their forefathers to give them, and you must divide it among them as their inheritance. The LORD himself goes before you and will be with you; he will never leave you nor forsake you. Do not be afraid; do not be discouraged."

Deuteronomy 31:7, 8

[Jesus] spoke to them and said, "Take courage! It is I. Don't be afraid."

Mark 6:50b

•*Dedication*

Are they servants of Christ? (I am out of my mind to talk like this.) I am more. I have worked much harder, been in prison more frequently, been flogged more severely, and been exposed to death again and again. Five times I received from the Jews the forty lashes minus one. Three times I was beaten with rods, once I was stoned, three times I was shipwrecked, I spent a night and a day in the open sea, I

23

have been constantly on the move. I have been in danger from rivers, in danger from bandits, in danger from my own countrymen, in danger from Gentiles; in danger in the city, in danger in the country, in danger at sea; and in danger from false brothers. I have labored and toiled and have often gone without sleep; I have known hunger and thirst and have often gone without food; I have been cold and naked. Besides everything else, I face daily the pressure of my concern for all the churches. Who is weak, and I do not feel weak? Who is led into sin, and I do not inwardly burn?

If I must boast, I will boast of the things that show my weakness. The God and Father of the Lord Jesus, who is to be praised forever, knows that I am not lying.

II Corinthians 11:23-31

• *Commitment*

Commit your way to the LORD; trust in him and he will do this.

Psalm 37:5

Paul and Barnabas appointed elders for them in each church and, with prayer and fasting, committed them to the Lord, in whom they had put their trust. After going through Pisidia, they came into Pamphylia, and when they had preached the word in Perga, they went down to Attalia. From Attalia they sailed back to Antioch, where they had been committed to the grace of God for the work they had now completed.

Acts 14:23-26

• *Initiative*

One day Jonathan son of Saul said to the young man bearing his armor, "Come, let's go over to the Philistine outpost on the other side." But he did not tell his father. Jonathan said to his young armor-bearer, "Come, let's go over to the outpost of those uncircumcised fellows. Perhaps the LORD will act in our behalf. Nothing can hinder the LORD from saving, whether by many or by few."

"Do all that you have in mind," his armor-bearer said. "Go ahead; I am with you heart and soul."

I Samuel 14:1, 6, 7

Some time later Joash decided to restore the temple of the LORD. He called together the priests and Levites and said to them, "Go to the towns of Judah and collect the money due annually from all Israel, to repair the temple of your God. Do it now." But the Levites did not act at once.

II Chronicles 24:4, 5

Jesus got up and went with him, and so did his disciples.

25

Just then a woman who had been subject to bleeding for twelve years came up behind him and touched the edge of his cloak. She said to herself, "If I only touch his cloak, I will be healed."

Jesus turned and saw her. "Take heart, daughter," he said, "your faith has healed you." And the woman was healed from that moment.

Matthew 9:19-22

Prepare for Opposition to Your New Family's Biblical Values

Blessed is the man who perseveres under trial, because when he has stood the test, he will receive the crown of life that God has promised to those who love him.

James 1:12

"If the world hates you, keep in mind that it hated me first. If you belonged to the world, it would love you as its own. As it is, you do not belong to the world, but I have chosen you out of the world. That is why the world hates you."

John 15:18, 19

If you are insulted because of the name of Christ, you are blessed, for the Spirit of glory and of God rests on you. If you suffer, it should not be as a murderer or thief or any other kind of criminal, or even as a meddler. However, if you suffer as a Christian, do not be ashamed, but praise God that you bear that name.

I Peter 4:14, 15

These [trials] have come so that your faith—of greater worth than gold, which perishes even though refined by fire—may be proved genuine and may result in praise, glory and honor when Jesus Christ is revealed.

I Peter 1:7

FOR PERSONAL PRAYER:

Lord, I've started on a new, exciting adventure. As I approach the twists and turns in the road ahead, grant me strength to persevere during the times when the road is a bit bumpy. And remind me to lift up praise for the blessings that come my way on this journey. Amen.

CHAPTER 2

'Am I ready to take on my new roles and responsibilites?'

I wish my parents would have done a better job of preparing me for married life," said Jane. "My mother always spoke so romantically about marriage, telling me all about her dating years with Dad. But the practical challenges of 'making it work,' year after year, kind of got left out.

"I know that being married means seeing myself in a whole new light. Already I've struggled a bit with the tremendous responsibility of caring about another person's happiness just as much as I care about my own. I'm beginning to see that being in love takes some courage."

FOR MEMORY:
Submit to one another out of reverence for Christ.

Ephesians 5:21

FOR SILENT REFLECTION:

- *What are some of the joys, benefits, challenges, and tasks of my new role? Which did I anticipate before marriage? Which are surprising to me now?*

- *In what ways do I carry out my responsibility to appreciate and encourage my mate?*

- *How does my understanding of my roles and responsibilities differ from my spouse's understanding? Have we talked about this? What adjustments could we make in order to work together more smoothly?*

- *In what ways do we expect our roles to change over the years? How will we prepare ourselves for this growth in our relationship?*

Your New Roles and Responsibilities

• *Live in Cooperation and Unselfishness*
Carry each other's burdens, and in this way you will
fulfill the law of Christ.

Galatians 6:2

"Again, I tell you that if two of you on earth agree
about anything you ask for, it will be done for you
by my Father in heaven. For where two or three
come together in my name, there am I with them."

Matthew 18:19, 20

"For I have come down from heaven not to do my
will but to do the will of him who sent me."

John 6:38

• *Be Honest in All Your Dealings with One Another*
Do not steal.
Do not lie.
Do not deceive one another.

Leviticus 19:11

Keep me from deceitful ways;
be gracious to me through your law.
I have chosen the way of truth;
I have set my heart on your laws.
I hold fast to your statutes, O LORD;

31

do not let me be put to shame.
I run in the path of your commands,
for you have set my heart free.
Teach me, O LORD, to follow your decrees;
then I will keep them to the end.
Give me understanding,
and I will keep your law and obey it with all my
heart.
Direct me in the path of your commands,
for there I find delight.
Turn my heart toward your statutes
and not toward selfish gain.
Turn my eyes away from worthless things;
preserve my life according to your word.

Psalm 119:29-37

Do not lie to each other, since you have taken off
your old self with its practices and have put on the
new self, which is being renewed in knowledge in
the image of its Creator.

Colossians 3:9, 10

• *Trust God Together for All You Need*

"I tell you, do not worry about your life, what you
will eat or drink; or about your body, what you will
wear. Is not life more important than food, and the
body more important than clothes? Look at the birds
of the air; they do not sow or reap or store away in

barns, and yet your heavenly Father feeds them. Are you not much more valuable than they?

"Who of you by worrying can add a single hour to his life? And why do you worry about clothes? See how the lilies of the field grow. They do not labor or spin. Yet I tell you that not even Solomon in all his splendor was dressed like one of these. If that is how God clothes the grass of the field, which is here today and tomorrow is thrown into the fire, will he not much more clothe you, O you of little faith? So do not worry, saying, 'What shall we eat?' or 'What shall we drink?' or 'What shall we wear?' For the pagans run after all these things, and your heavenly Father knows that you need them. But seek first his kingdom and his righteousness, and all these things will be given to you as well. Therefore do not worry about tomorrow, for tomorrow will worry about itself. Each day has enough trouble of its own."

Matthew 6:25-34

Do not be anxious about anything, but in everything, by prayer and petition, with thanksgiving, present your requests to God. And the peace of God, which transcends all understanding, will guard your hearts and your minds in Christ Jesus. . . . I am not saying this because I am in need, for I have learned to be content whatever the circumstances. I know what it is to be in need, and I know what it is to have plen-

33

ty. I have learned the secret of being content in any and every situation, whether well fed or hungry, whether living in plenty or in want.

Philippians 4:6-12

Husbands, Love and Adore Your Wives

A wife of noble character who can find?
She is worth far more than rubies.
Her husband has full confidence in her
and lacks nothing of value.
She brings him good, not harm,
all the days of her life.
She selects wool and flax
and works with eager hands.
She is like the merchant ships,
bringing her food from afar.
She gets up while it is still dark;
she provides food for her family
and portions for her servant girls.
She considers a field and buys it;
out of her earnings she plants a vineyard.
She sets about her work vigorously;
her arms are strong for her tasks.
She sees that her trading is profitable,
and her lamp does not go out at night.
In her hand she holds the distaff
and grasps the spindle with her fingers.

She opens her arms to the poor
and extends her hands to the needy.
When it snows, she has no fear for her household;
for all of them are clothed in scarlet.
She makes coverings for her bed;
she is clothed in fine linen and purple.
Her husband is respected at the city gate,
where he takes his seat among the elders of the land.
She makes linen garments and sells them,
and supplies the merchants with sashes.
She is clothed with strength and dignity;
she can laugh at the days to come.
She speaks with wisdom,
and faithful instruction is on her tongue.
She watches over the affairs of her household
and does not eat the bread of idleness.
Her children arise and call her blessed;
her husband also, and he praises her:
"Many women do noble things,
but you surpass them all."

Proverbs 31:10-29

How beautiful you are, my darling!
Oh, how beautiful! Your eyes behind your veil are
doves.

Song of Songs 4:1a

Submit to one another out of reverence for Christ. . . .

Husbands, love your wives, just as Christ loved the church and gave himself up for her to make her holy, cleansing her by the washing with water through the word, and to present her to himself as a radiant church, without stain or wrinkle or any other blemish, but holy and blameless. In this same way, husbands ought to love their wives as their own bodies. He who loves his wife loves himself. After all, no one ever hated his own body, but he feeds and cares for it, just as Christ does the church—for we are members of his body. "For this reason a man will leave his father and mother and be united to his wife, and the two will become one flesh." This is a profound mystery—but I am talking about Christ and the church. However, each one of you also must love his wife as he loves himself.

Ephesians 5:21-33a

Husbands, in the same way be considerate as you live with your wives, and treat them with respect as the weaker partner and as heirs with you of the gracious gift of life, so that nothing will hinder your prayers.

I Peter 3:7

• Some Faithful Husbands

Isaac

Now Isaac had come from Beer Lahai Roi, for he was

living in the Negev. He went out to the field one evening to meditate, and as he looked up, he saw camels approaching. Rebekah also looked up and saw Isaac. She got down from her camel and asked the servant, "Who is that man in the field coming to meet us?"

"He is my master," the servant answered. So she took her veil and covered herself.

Then the servant told Isaac all he had done. Isaac brought her into the tent of his mother Sarah, and he married Rebekah. So she became his wife, and he loved her.

Genesis 24:62-67a

Hosea

When the LORD began to speak through Hosea, the LORD said to him, "Go, take to yourself an adulterous wife and children of unfaithfulness, because the land is guilty of the vilest adultery in departing from the LORD." So he married Gomer daughter of Diblaim.

"She will chase after her lovers but not catch them; she will look for them but not find them. Then she will say, 'I will go back to my husband as at first, for then I was better off than now.'

"Therefore I [the Lord] am now going to allure her; I will lead her into the desert and speak tenderly to her. There I will give her back her vineyards, and will make the Valley of Achor a door of hope. There

37

she will sing as in the days of her youth, as in the day she came up out of Egypt. "In that day," declares the LORD, "you will call me 'my husband'; you will no longer call me 'my master.' I will remove the names of the Baals from her lips; no longer will their names be invoked.

In that day I will make a covenant for them with the beasts of the field and the birds of the air and the creatures that move along the ground. Bow and sword and battle I will abolish from the land, so that all may lie down in safety. I will betroth you to me forever; I will betroth you in righteousness and justice, in love and compassion. I will betroth you in faithfulness, and you will acknowledge the LORD.

"I will plant her for myself in the land; I will show my love to the one I called 'Not my loved one.' I will say to those called 'Not my people,' 'You are my people'; and they will say, 'You are my God.'"

The LORD said to me, "Go, show your love to your wife again, though she is loved by another and is an adulteress. Love her as the LORD loves the Israelites, though they turn to other gods and love the sacred raisin cakes."

So I bought her for fifteen shekels of silver and about a homer and a lethek of barley. Then I told her, "You are to live with me many days; you must not be a prostitute or be intimate with any man, and I will live with you."

For the Israelites will live many days without king or prince, without sacrifice or sacred stones, without ephod or idol. Afterward the Israelites will return and seek the LORD their God and David their king. They will come trembling to the LORD and to his blessings in the last days.

Hosea 1:2-3a; 2:7, 14-20, 23; 3:1-5

Joseph

This is how the birth of Jesus Christ came about: His mother Mary was pledged to be married to Joseph, but before they came together, she was found to be with child through the Holy Spirit. Because Joseph her husband was a righteous man and did not want to expose her to public disgrace, he had in mind to divorce her quietly.

But after he had considered this, an angel of the Lord appeared to him in a dream and said, "Joseph son of David, do not be afraid to take Mary home as your wife, because what is conceived in her is from the Holy Spirit. She will give birth to a son, and you are to give him the name Jesus, because he will save his people from their sins."

All this took place to fulfill what the Lord had said through the prophet: "The virgin will be with child and will give birth to a son, and they will call him Immanuel"—which means, "God with us."

When Joseph woke up, he did what the angel of

the Lord had commanded him and took Mary home as his wife. But he had no union with her until she gave birth to a son. And he gave him the name Jesus.

Matthew 1:18-25

•*An Unreasonable, Oppressive Husband*

But when the attendants delivered the king's command, Queen Vashti refused to come. Then the king became furious and burned with anger. . . .

"According to law, what must be done to Queen Vashti?" he asked. "She has not obeyed the command of King Xerxes that the eunuchs have taken to her."

Then Memucan replied in the presence of the king and the nobles, "Queen Vashti has done wrong, not only against the king but also against all the nobles and the peoples of all the provinces of King Xerxes. For the queen's conduct will become known to all the women, and so they will despise their husbands and say, 'King Xerxes commanded Queen Vashti to be brought before him, but she would not come.' This very day the Persian and Median women of the nobility who have heard about the queen's conduct will respond to all the king's nobles in the same way. There will be no end of disrespect and discord.

"Therefore, if it pleases the king, let him issue a royal decree and let it be written in the laws of Persia and Media, which cannot be repealed, that Vashti is never again to enter the presence of King Xerxes. Also let the king give her royal position to someone else who is better than she. Then when the king's edict is proclaimed throughout all his vast realm, all the women will respect their husbands, from the least to the greatest."

The king and his nobles were pleased with this advice, so the king did as Memucan proposed. He sent dispatches to all parts of the kingdom, to each province in its own script and to each people in its own language, proclaiming in each people's tongue that every man should be ruler over his own household.

Esther 1:12-22

Wives, Be Inspired by Women of Heroic Spirit

• *Miriam*

Then Miriam the prophetess, Aaron's sister, took a tambourine in her hand, and all the women followed her, with tambourines and dancing. Miriam sang to them: "Sing to the LORD, for he is highly exalted. The horse and its rider he has hurled into the sea."

Exodus 15:20

• *Deborah*

Deborah, a prophetess, the wife of Lappidoth, was leading Israel at that time. She held court under the

41

Palm of Deborah between Ramah and Bethel in the hill country of Ephraim, and the Israelites came to her to have their disputes decided.

She sent for Barak son of Abinoam from Kedesh in Naphtali and said to him, "The LORD, the God of Israel, commands you: 'Go, take with you ten thousand men of Naphtali and Zebulun and lead the way to Mount Tabor. I will lure Sisera, the commander of Jabin's army, with his chariots and his troops to the Kishon River and give him into your hands.'"

Barak said to her, "If you go with me, I will go; but if you don't go with me, I won't go."

"Very well," Deborah said, "I will go with you. But because of the way you are going about this, the honor will not be yours, for the LORD will hand Sisera over to a woman."

So Deborah went with Barak to Kedesh, where he summoned Zebulun and Naphtali. Ten thousand men followed him, and Deborah also went with him. Now Heber the Kenite had left the other Kenites, the descendants of Hobab, Moses' brother-in-law, and pitched his tent by the great tree in Zaanannim near Kedesh. When they told Sisera that Barak son of Abinoam had gone up to Mount Tabor, Sisera gathered together his nine hundred iron chariots and all the men with him, from Harosheth Haggoyim to the Kishon River.

Then Deborah said to Barak, "Go! This is the day

the LORD has given Sisera into your hands. Has not the LORD gone ahead of you?" So Barak went down Mount Tabor, followed by ten thousand men.

Judges 4:4-14

•*A Greek Woman Who Bravely Persisted*

Jesus left that place and went to the vicinity of Tyre. He entered a house and did not want anyone to know it; yet he could not keep his presence secret. In fact, as soon as she heard about him, a woman whose little daughter was possessed by an evil spirit came and fell at his feet.

The woman was a Greek, born in Syrian Phoenicia. She begged Jesus to drive the demon out of her daughter. "First let the children eat all they want," he told her, "for it is not right to take the children's bread and toss it to their dogs."

"Yes, Lord," she replied, "but even the dogs under the table eat the children's crumbs."

Then he told her, "For such a reply, you may go; the demon has left your daughter." She went home and found her child lying on the bed, and the demon gone.

Mark 7:24-30

•*Pilate's Wife*

While Pilate was sitting on the judge's seat, his wife sent him this message: "Don't have anything to do

43

with that innocent man, for I have suffered a great deal today in a dream because of him."

Matthew 27:19

• *Women at the Cross*

Among them were Mary Magdalene, Mary the mother of James and Joses, and the mother of Zebedee's sons. As evening approached, there came a rich man from Arimathea, named Joseph, who had himself become a disciple of Jesus. . . . Joseph took [Jesus'] body . . . and placed it in his own new tomb that he had cut out of the rock. He rolled a big stone in front of the entrance to the tomb and went away. Mary Magdalene and the other Mary were sitting there opposite the tomb.

Matthew 27:56-61

After the Sabbath, at dawn on the first day of the week, Mary Magdalene and the other Mary went to look at the tomb.

Matthew 28:1

Near the cross of Jesus stood his mother, his mother's sister, Mary the wife of Clopas, and Mary Magdalene.

John 19:25

• *Lydia*

One of those listening was a woman named Lydia, a

dealer in purple cloth from the city of Thyatira, who was a worshiper of God. The Lord opened her heart to respond to Paul's message. When she and the members of her household were baptized, she invited us to her home. "If you consider me a believer in the Lord," she said, "come and stay at my house." And she persuaded us.

Acts 16:14, 15

• *Priscilla and Aquila*

There he met a Jew named Aquila, a native of Pontus, who had recently come from Italy with his wife Priscilla, because Claudius had ordered all the Jews to leave Rome. Paul went to see them.

Meanwhile a Jew named Apollos, a native of Alexandria, came to Ephesus. He was a learned man, with a thorough knowledge of the Scriptures. He had been instructed in the way of the Lord, and he spoke with great fervor and taught about Jesus accurately, though he knew only the baptism of John. He began to speak boldly in the synagogue. When Priscilla and Aquila heard him, they invited him to their home and explained to him the way of God more adequately.

Acts 18:2, 24-26

• *Manoah's Wife*

A certain man of Zorah, named Manoah, from the clan of the Danites, had a wife who was sterile and remained childless. The angel of the LORD appeared to her and said, "You are sterile and childless, but you are going to conceive and have a son. Now see to it that you drink no wine or other fermented drink and that you do not eat anything unclean, because you will conceive and give birth to a son. No razor may be used on his head, because the boy is to be a Nazirite, set apart to God from birth, and he will begin the deliverance of Israel from the hands of the Philistines."

Then the woman went to her husband and told him, "A man of God came to me. He looked like an angel of God, very awesome. I didn't ask him where he came from, and he didn't tell me his name. But he said to me, 'You will conceive and give birth to a son. Now then, drink no wine or other fermented drink and do not eat anything unclean, because the boy will be a Nazirite of God from birth until the day of his death.'"

Then Manoah prayed to the LORD: "O Lord, I beg you, let the man of God you sent to us come again to teach us how to bring up the boy who is to be born."

God heard Manoah, and the angel of God came again to the woman while she was out in the field; but her husband Manoah was not with her.

The woman hurried to tell her husband, "He's here! The man who appeared to me the other day!" Manoah got up and followed his wife. When he came to the man, he said, "Are you the one who talked to my wife?"

"I am," he said. So Manoah asked him, "When your words are fulfilled, what is to be the rule for the boy's life and work?"

The angel of the LORD answered, "Your wife must do all that I have told her. She must not eat anything that comes from the grapevine, nor drink any wine or other fermented drink nor eat anything unclean. She must do everything I have commanded her." The woman gave birth to a boy and named him Samson. He grew and the LORD blessed him, and the Spirit of the LORD began to stir him.

Judges 13:2-14, 24, 25a

• *Wives of Sincere Faith*

Paul, an apostle of Christ Jesus by the will of God, according to the promise of life that is in Christ Jesus, To Timothy, my dear son: Grace, mercy and peace from God the Father and Christ Jesus our Lord. I thank God, whom I serve, as my forefathers did, with a clear conscience, as night and day I constantly remember you in my prayers. Recalling your tears, I long to see you, so that I may be filled with joy. I have been reminded of your sincere faith, which first lived in your grandmother Lois and in your mother Eunice and, I am persuaded, now lives in you also.

II Timothy 1:1-5

47

FOR PERSONAL PRAYER:

Father, it is good to take on new roles and responsibilities. But it is also a bit fearful. Bring into my life wise people who have been there before—people who can show me the ropes. Amen.

Chapter 3

'How will we handle our conflicts?'

Tony was taught by his parents that fighting is always bad," said Alice. "So every time it looks like we might have a disagreement, he just clams up.

"I don't mind keeping things smooth and calm in our household, but I definitely think we need to talk about the things that make us uncomfortable. Avoiding those problems just makes them get bigger, out of sight, until they burst into the open, full-grown."

FOR MEMORY:

Speaking the truth in love, we will in all things grow up into him who is the Head, that is, Christ.

Ephesians 4:15

FOR SILENT REFLECTION:

- *What were the attitudes about conflict that I received from my family?*

- *How do those attitudes come through in the way I approach marital conflicts?*

- *What can I do to take the first step toward resolving a current conflict?*

- *In what ways could I open up and be more vulnerable, even when I feel threatened?*

Do You Communicate Lovingly?

Speaking the truth in love, we will in all things grow up into him who is the Head, that is, Christ. From him the whole body, joined and held together by every supporting ligament, grows and builds itself up in love, as each part does its work.

Ephesians 4:15, 16

Speak to one another with psalms, hymns and spiritual songs. Sing and make music in your heart to the Lord, always giving thanks to God the Father for everything, in the name of our Lord Jesus Christ.

Ephesians 5:19, 20

Develop Attitudes That Will Help You Resolve Your Conflicts

Do not conform any longer to the pattern of this world, but be transformed by the renewing of your mind. Then you will be able to test and approve what God's will is—his good, pleasing and perfect will.

Romans 12:2

• *Learn to Control Your Anger*
A quick-tempered man does foolish things,
and a crafty man is hated.

Proverbs 14:17

51

A patient man has great understanding,
but a quick-tempered man displays folly.

Proverbs 14:29

From that day Saul kept David with him and did not let him return to his father's house. The next day an evil spirit from God came forcefully upon Saul. He was prophesying in his house, while David was playing the harp, as he usually did. Saul had a spear in his hand and he hurled it, saying to himself, "I'll pin David to the wall." But David eluded him twice. Saul's anger flared up at Jonathan and he said to him, "You son of a perverse and rebellious woman! Don't I know that you have sided with the son of Jesse to your own shame and to the shame of the mother who bore you? As long as the son of Jesse lives on this earth, neither you nor your kingdom will be established. Now send and bring him to me, for he must die!"

"Why should he be put to death? What has he done?" Jonathan asked his father.

But Saul hurled his spear at him to kill him. Then Jonathan knew that his father intended to kill David. Jonathan got up from the table in fierce anger; on that second day of the month he did not eat, because he was grieved at his father's shameful treatment of David.

I Samuel 18:2, 10, 11; 20:30-34

Better a patient man than a warrior,
a man who controls his temper than one who takes a
city.

Proverbs 16:32

•*Constantly Seek Wisdom from God*
Let the wise listen and add to their learning,
and let the discerning get guidance.

Proverbs 1:5

For the LORD gives wisdom,
and from his mouth come knowledge and understanding.

Proverbs 2:6

Blessed is the man who finds wisdom,
the man who gains understanding.

Proverbs 3:13

The fear of the LORD is the beginning of wisdom,
and knowledge of the Holy One is understanding.

Proverbs 9:10

He who gets wisdom loves his own soul;
he who cherishes understanding prospers.

Proverbs 19:8

Wisdom is better than folly,

just as light is better than darkness.

Ecclesiastes 2:13

When Jesus spoke again to the people, he said, "I am the light of the world. Whoever follows me will never walk in darkness, but will have the light of life."

John 8:12

But God has revealed it to us by his Spirit. The Spirit searches all things, even the deep things of God.

I Corinthians 2:10

The man without the Spirit does not accept the things that come from the Spirit of God, for they are foolishness to him, and he cannot understand them, because they are spiritually discerned. The spiritual man makes judgments about all things, but he himself is not subject to any man's judgment.

I Corinthians 2:14, 15

We know also that the Son of God has come and has given us understanding, so that we may know him who is true. . . . He is the true God and eternal life.

I John 5:20

•*Approach Your Spouse with a Servant Attitude*

Your attitude should be the same as that of Christ Jesus:

Who, being in very nature God,
did not consider equality with God something to be
grasped,
but made himself nothing,
taking the very nature of a servant,
being made in human likeness.
And being found in appearance as a man,
he humbled himself and became obedient to death—
even death on a cross!

Therefore God exalted him to the highest place
and gave him the name that is above every name,
that at the name of Jesus every knee should bow,
in heaven and on earth and under the earth,
and every tongue confess that Jesus Christ is Lord,
to the glory of God the Father.

Therefore, my dear friends, as you have always obeyed—not only in my presence, but now much more in my absence—continue to work out your salvation with fear and trembling, for it is God who works in you to will and to act according to his good purpose.

Do everything without complaining or arguing, so that you may become blameless and pure, children of God without fault in a crooked and depraved generation, in which you shine like stars in the universe as you hold out the word of life—in order that I may boast on the day of Christ that I did not run or labor for nothing.

Philippians 2:5-16

Recognize the Feelings That Make You Vulnerable to Conflict

• *Do You Feel Discouraged?*

I am feeble and utterly crushed;
I groan in anguish of heart.
All my longings lie open before you,
O Lord; my sighing is not hidden from you.
My heart pounds, my strength fails me;
even the light has gone from my eyes.
My friends and companions avoid me because of my
wounds;
my neighbors stay far away.

Psalm 38:8-11

For my days vanish like smoke;
my bones burn like glowing embers.
My heart is blighted and withered like grass;
I forget to eat my food.
Because of my loud groaning
I am reduced to skin and bones.
I am like a desert owl,
like an owl among the ruins.
I lie awake;
I have become like a bird alone on a roof.
All day long my enemies taunt me;
those who rail against me use my name as a curse.
For I eat ashes as my food

and mingle my drink with tears
because of your great wrath,
for you have taken me up and thrown me aside.
My days are like the evening shadow;
I wither away like grass.

Psalm 102:3-11

My tears have been my food day and night,
while men say to me all day long, "Where is your
God?

Psalm 42:3

Record my lament; list my tears on your scroll—
are they not in your record?

Psalm 56:8

The churning inside me never stops;
days of suffering confront me.

Job 30:27

Hear my prayer, O LORD,
listen to my cry for help; be not deaf to my weeping.
For I dwell with you as an alien,
a stranger, as all my fathers were.

Psalm 39:12

•*Do You Feel Bitter about Past Hurts?*
What misery is mine! I am like one who gathers sum-

57

mer fruit at the gleaning of the vineyard; there is no
cluster of grapes to eat, none of the early figs that I
crave.

Micah 7:1

Then Jesus told his disciples a parable to show them
that they should always pray and not give up. He
said: "In a certain town there was a judge who neither feared God nor cared about men. And there was
a widow in that town who kept coming to him with
the plea, 'Grant me justice against my adversary.'

"For some time he refused. But finally he said to
himself, 'Even though I don't fear God or care about
men, yet because this widow keeps bothering me, I
will see that she gets justice, so that she won't even-
tually wear me out with her coming!'"

And the Lord said, "Listen to what the unjust judge
says. And will not God bring about justice for his
chosen ones, who cry out to him day and night? Will
he keep putting them off?"

Luke 18:1-7

"In your anger do not sin": Do not let the sun go
down while you are still angry.

Ephesians 4:26

• *Do You Feel Ashamed or Rejected?*
My disgrace is before me all day long,

58

and my face is covered with shame.

Psalm 44:15

You know how I am scorned,
disgraced and shamed; all my enemies are before
you.

Psalm 69:19

I sought the LORD, and he answered me;
he delivered me from all my fears.
Those who look to him are radiant;
their faces are never covered with shame.

Psalm 34:4, 5

In you, O LORD, I have taken refuge;
let me never be put to shame.

Psalm 71:1

Instead of their shame my people will receive a
double portion,
and instead of disgrace they will rejoice in their
inheritance;
and so they will inherit a double portion in their
land,
and everlasting joy will be theirs.

Isaiah 61:7

You will have plenty to eat, until you are full,

and you will praise the name of the LORD your God,
who has worked wonders for you;
never again will my people be shamed.
Then you will know that I am in Israel,
that I am the LORD your God,
and that there is no other;
never again will my people be shamed.

Joel 2:26, 27

As it is written: "See, I lay in Zion a stone that causes
men to stumble and a rock that makes them fall, and
the one who trusts in him will never be put to shame."

Romans 9:33

•*Do You Feel Guilty or Condemned?*

Then the LORD said to Satan, "Have you considered
my servant Job? There is no one on earth like him;
he is blameless and upright, a man who fears God
and shuns evil."

"Does Job fear God for nothing?" Satan replied.
"Have you not put a hedge around him and his
household and everything he has? You have blessed
the work of his hands, so that his flocks and herds
are spread throughout the land."

Job 1:8-10

Even if I were innocent, my mouth would condemn
me;

60

if I were blameless, it would pronounce me guilty.
Although I am blameless, I have no concern for
myself;
I despise my own life.

Job 9:20, 21

Are you so foolish? After beginning with the Spirit,
are you now trying to attain your goal by human
effort? Have you suffered so much for nothing—if it
really was for nothing?

Galatians 3:3, 4

Jesus, full of the Holy Spirit, returned from the Jor-
dan and was led by the Spirit in the desert, where for
forty days he was tempted by the devil. He ate nothing during those days, and at the end of them he
was hungry. The devil said to him, "If you are the
Son of God, tell this stone to become bread."

Jesus answered, "It is written: 'Man does not live
on bread alone.'" The devil led him up to a high
place and showed him in an instant all the kingdoms
of the world. And he said to him, "I will give you all
their authority and splendor, for it has been given to
me, and I can give it to anyone I want to." When the
devil had finished all this tempting, he left him until
an opportune time.

Luke 4:1-6, 13

61

Be self-controlled and alert. Your enemy the devil prowls around like a roaring lion looking for someone to devour.

I Peter 5:8

When you were dead in your sins and in the uncircumcision of your sinful nature, God made you alive with Christ. He forgave us all our sins, having canceled the written code, with its regulations, that was against us and that stood opposed to us; he took it away, nailing it to the cross. And having disarmed the powers and authorities, he made a public spectacle of them, triumphing over them by the cross.

Therefore do not let anyone judge you by what you eat or drink, or with regard to a religious festival, a New Moon celebration or a Sabbath day. These are a shadow of the things that were to come; the reality, however, is found in Christ. Do not let anyone who delights in false humility and the worship of angels disqualify you for the prize. Such a person goes into great detail about what he has seen, and his unspiritual mind puffs him up with idle notions. He has lost connection with the Head, from whom the whole body, supported and held together by its ligaments and sinews, grows as God causes it to grow.

Since you died with Christ to the basic principles of this world, why, as though you still belonged to it, do you submit to its rules: "Do not handle! Do not taste! Do not touch!"? These are all destined to perish with use, because they are based on human commands and teachings. Such regulations indeed have an appearance of wisdom, with their self-imposed worship, their false humility and their harsh treatment of the body, but they lack any value in restraining sensual indulgence.

Colossians 2:13-23

God Will Carry You through This Conflict

But you, O God, do see trouble and grief;
you consider it to take it in hand.
The victim commits himself to you;
you are the helper of the fatherless.

Psalm 10:14

My flesh and my heart may fail,
but God is the strength of my heart and my portion forever.

Psalm 73:26

Unless the LORD had given me help,
I would soon have dwelt in the silence of death.
When I said, "My foot is slipping,"
your love, O LORD, supported me.
When anxiety was great within me,

63

your consolation brought joy to my soul.

Psalm 94:17-19

The Sovereign LORD has given me an instructed
tongue,
to know the word that sustains the weary.
He wakens me morning by morning,
wakens my ear to listen like one being taught.
The Sovereign LORD has opened my ears,
and I have not been rebellious;
I have not drawn back.
I offered my back to those who beat me,
my cheeks to those who pulled out my beard;
I did not hide my face from mocking and spitting.
Because the Sovereign LORD helps me,
I will not be disgraced. Therefore have I set my face
like flint,
and I know I will not be put to shame.
He who vindicates me is near.
Who then will bring charges against me?
Let us face each other! Who is my accuser?
Let him confront me!
It is the Sovereign LORD who helps me.
Who is he that will condemn me?
They will all wear out like a garment; the moths will
eat them up.
Who among you fears the LORD
and obeys the word of his servant?

Let him who walks in the dark, who has no light, trust in the name of the LORD and rely on his God.

Isaiah 50:4-10

"Come to me, all you who are weary and burdened, and I will give you rest. Take my yoke upon you and learn from me, for I am gentle and humble in heart, and you will find rest for your souls. For my yoke is easy and my burden is light."

Matthew 11:28-30

"Do not let your hearts be troubled. Trust in God; trust also in me. Peace I leave with you; my peace I give you. I do not give to you as the world gives. Do not let your hearts be troubled and do not be afraid."

John 14:1, 27

We are hard pressed on every side, but not crushed; perplexed, but not in despair; persecuted, but not abandoned; struck down, but not destroyed. Therefore we do not lose heart. Though outwardly we are wasting away, yet inwardly we are being renewed day by day. For our light and momentary troubles are achieving for us an eternal glory that far outweighs them all. So we fix our eyes not on what is seen, but on what is unseen. For what is seen is temporary, but what is unseen is eternal.

II Corinthians 4:8, 9, 16-18

For the grace of God that brings salvation has appeared to all men. It teaches us to say "No" to ungodliness and worldly passions, and to live self-controlled, upright and godly lives in this present age, while we wait for the blessed hope—the glorious appearing of our great God and Savior, Jesus Christ, who gave himself for us to redeem us from all wickedness and to purify for himself a people that are his very own, eager to do what is good.

Titus 2:11-14

In this you greatly rejoice, though now for a little while you may have had to suffer grief in all kinds of trials.

I Peter 1:6

FOR PERSONAL PRAYER:

Lord Jesus, help me learn how to give my love in a way that honors my own needs while trying to meet another's. Teach me the wisdom of vulnerability and unselfishness in this relationship, even during the times when I sense that my "rights" are being violated. Amen.

CHAPTER 4

'How will I deal with my unrealistic expectations?'

Brian said, "I expected things to be a little different. A case in point: I assumed that I would keep all my old friends and still hang around the same old places in my free time. I'd just have a wife to go with me now.

"But that's not how things have turned out. For one thing, my old friends don't seem so interested in me anymore; I'm like this strange, new creature. And my wife wants me home most of the time, so I don't get out much anyway.

"I guess I'm having to learn how to let go of the single life and focus on my new situation. That's okay; it's a good place to be. Just different."

> **FOR MEMORY:**
> Delight yourself in the LORD
> and he will give you the desires of your
> heart.
>
> *Psalm 37:4*

FOR SILENT REFLECTION:

- *What were my biggest expectations for married life?*

- *How have my expectations been fulfilled? In what ways have some of them been thwarted? How do I handle my disappointments?*

- *Which of my expectations have been unrealistic? Which could be fulfilled if I worked at changing my circumstances in some way?*

- *In which areas do I need to develop an attitude of greater acceptance?*

Feeling Loss after Giving Up the Single Life?

• *God Stays Right with Me When Commitment Wanes*

Call upon me in the day of trouble;
I will deliver you, and you will honor me.

Psalm 50:15

Cast your cares on the LORD and he will sustain you;
he will never let the righteous fall.

Psalm 55:22

And I will ask the Father, and he will give you
another Counselor to be with you forever—the Spirit
of truth. The world cannot accept him, because it
neither sees him nor knows him. But you know him,
for he lives with you and will be in you. I will not
leave you as orphans; I will come to you. Before
long, the world will not see me anymore, but you
will see me. Because I live, you also will live.

John 14:16-19

But Zion said, "The LORD has forsaken me, the Lord
has forgotten me."

Can a mother forget the baby at her breast and
have no compassion on the child she has borne?
Though she may forget, I will not forget you!

Isaiah 49:14, 15

Who is a God like you,

69

who pardons sin and forgives the transgression
of the remnant of his inheritance?
You do not stay angry forever but delight to show
mercy.
You will again have compassion on us;
you will tread our sins underfoot
and hurl all our iniquities into the depths of the sea.

Micah 7:18, 19

Therefore, brothers, since we have confidence to
enter the Most Holy Place by the blood of Jesus, by a
new and living way opened for us through the cur-
tain, that is, his body, and since we have a great
priest over the house of God, let us draw near to
God with a sincere heart in full assurance of faith,
having our hearts sprinkled to cleanse us from a
guilty conscience and having our bodies washed
with pure water.

Hebrews 10:19-22

In this way, love is made complete among us so that
we will have confidence on the day of judgment,
because in this world we are like him. There is no
fear in love. But perfect love drives out fear, because
fear has to do with punishment. The one who fears
is not made perfect in love.

I John 4:17, 18

• *He Helps Me Find Contentment in Tough Circumstances*

LORD, you have assigned me my portion and my cup;
you have made my lot secure.
The boundary lines have fallen for me in pleasant places;
surely I have a delightful inheritance.

Psalm 16:5, 6

Delight yourself in the LORD
and he will give you the desires of your heart.

Psalm 37:4

Better a meal of vegetables where there is love
than a fattened calf with hatred.

Proverbs 15:17

By wisdom a house is built,
and through understanding it is established;
through knowledge its rooms
are filled with rare and beautiful treasures.

Proverbs 24:3, 4

The LORD will guide you always;
he will satisfy your needs in a sun-scorched land
and will strengthen your frame.
You will be like a well-watered garden,

71

like a spring whose waters never fail.

Isaiah 58:11

• *He Calls Me to Persevere during Trials*

But mark this: There will be terrible times in the last days. People will be lovers of themselves, lovers of money, boastful, proud, abusive, disobedient to their parents, ungrateful, unholy, without love, unforgiving, slanderous, without self-control, brutal, not lovers of the good, treacherous, rash, conceited, lovers of pleasure rather than lovers of God.

II Timothy 3:1-4

Therefore, prepare your minds for action; be self-controlled; set your hope fully on the grace to be given you when Jesus Christ is revealed. As obedient children, do not conform to the evil desires you had when you lived in ignorance. But just as he who called you is holy, so be holy in all you do; for it is written: "Be holy, because I am holy."

I Peter 1:13-16

"Anyone who does not carry his cross and follow me cannot be my disciple. Suppose one of you wants to build a tower. Will he not first sit down and estimate the cost to see if he has enough money to complete it? For if he lays the foundation and is not able to finish it, everyone who sees it will ridicule him, saying, 'This fellow began to build and was not able to finish.'

"Or suppose a king is about to go to war against another king. Will he not first sit down and consider whether he is able with ten thousand men to oppose the one coming against him with twenty thousand? If he is not able, he will send a delegation while the other is still a long way off and will ask for terms of peace. In the same way, any of you who does not give up everything he has cannot be my disciple.

"Salt is good, but if it loses its saltiness, how can it be made salty again? It is fit neither for the soil nor for the manure pile; it is thrown out.

"He who has ears to hear, let him hear."

Luke 14:27-35

Yet I am not ashamed, because I know whom I have believed, and am convinced that he is able to guard what I have entrusted to him for that day.

II Timothy 1:12b

• *He Promises a Place Where Loss Can Never Touch Me Again*

In my Father's house are many rooms; if it were not so, I would have told you. I am going there to prepare a place for you. And if I go and prepare a place for you, I will come back and take you to be with me that you also may be where I am.

John 14:2, 3

73

Then I saw a new heaven and a new earth, for the first heaven and the first earth had passed away, and there was no longer any sea. I saw the Holy City, the new Jerusalem, coming down out of heaven from God, prepared as a bride beautifully dressed for her husband. And I heard a loud voice from the throne saying, "Now the dwelling of God is with men, and he will live with them. They will be his people, and God himself will be with them and be their God. He will wipe every tear from their eyes. There will be no more death or mourning or crying or pain, for the old order of things has passed away."

Revelation 21:1-4

The city was laid out like a square, as long as it was wide. He measured the city with the rod and found it to be 12,000 stadia in length, and as wide and high as it is long. He measured its wall and it was 144 cubits thick, by man's measurement, which the angel was using. The wall was made of jasper, and the city of pure gold, as pure as glass. The foundations of the city walls were decorated with every kind of precious stone. The first foundation was jasper, the second sapphire, the third chalcedony, the fourth emerald, the fifth sardonyx, the sixth carnelian, the seventh chrysolite, the eighth beryl, the ninth topaz, the tenth chrysoprase, the eleventh jacinth, and the twelfth amethyst. The twelve gates were twelve pearls, each gate made of a single pearl. The great street of the city was of pure gold, like transparent glass.

I did not see a temple in the city, because the Lord God Almighty and the Lamb are its temple. The city does not need the sun or the moon to shine on it, for the glory of God gives it light, and the Lamb is its lamp. The nations will walk by its light, and the kings of the earth will bring their splendor into it. On no day will its gates ever be shut, for there will be no night there. The glory and honor of the nations will be brought into it. Nothing impure will ever enter it, nor will anyone who does what is shameful or deceitful, but only those whose names are written in the Lamb's book of life.

Revelation 21:16-27

• *He Promises an End to Loss Someday*
Even though I walk
through the valley of the shadow of death,
I will fear no evil, for you are with me;
your rod and your staff, they comfort me.
You prepare a table before me
in the presence of my enemies.
You anoint my head with oil;
my cup overflows.
Surely goodness and love will follow me
all the days of my life,

and I will dwell in the house of the LORD forever.

Psalm 23:4-6

I consider that our present sufferings are not worth comparing with the glory that will be revealed in us.

Romans 8:18

However, as it is written: "No eye has seen, no ear has heard, no mind has conceived what God has prepared for those who love him."

I Corinthians 2:9

Listen, I tell you a mystery: We will not all sleep, but we will all be changed—in a flash, in the twinkling of an eye, at the last trumpet. For the trumpet will sound, the dead will be raised imperishable, and we will be changed. For the perishable must clothe itself with the imperishable, and the mortal with immortality. When the perishable has been clothed with the imperishable, and the mortal with immortality, then the saying that is written will come true: "Death has been swallowed up in victory."

"Where, O death, is your victory? Where, O death, is your sting?"

I Corinthians 15:51-55

For the Lord himself will come down from heaven, with a loud command, with the voice of the archangel and with the trumpet call of God, and the dead in Christ will rise first. After that, we who are still alive and are left will be caught up together with them in the clouds to meet the Lord in the air. And so we will be with the Lord forever. Therefore encourage each other with these words.

I Thessalonians 4:16-18

But in keeping with his promise we are looking forward to a new heaven and a new earth, the home of righteousness.

II Peter 3:13

Nevertheless, I have this against you: You tolerate that woman Jezebel, who calls herself a prophetess. By her teaching she misleads my servants into sexual immorality and the eating of food sacrificed to idols.

Revelation 2:20

After this I looked and there before me was a great multitude that no one could count, from every nation, tribe, people and language, standing before the throne and in front of the Lamb. They . . . cried out in a loud voice: "Salvation belongs to our God, who sits on the throne, and to the Lamb."

All the angels were standing around the throne and around the elders and the four living creatures. They fell down on their faces before the throne and worshiped God, saying: "Amen! Praise and glory and wisdom and thanks and honor and power and strength be to our God for ever and ever. Amen!"

Then one of the elders asked me, "These in white robes—who are they, and where did they come from?" . . . And he said, "These are they who have come out of the great tribulation; they have washed their robes and made them white in the blood of the Lamb. Therefore, "they are before the throne of God and serve him day and night in his temple; and he who sits on the throne will spread his tent over them. Never again will they hunger; never again will they thirst. The sun will not beat upon them, nor any scorching heat. For the Lamb at the center of the throne will be their shepherd; he will lead them to springs of living water. And God will wipe away every tear from their eyes."

Revelation 7:9-17

Will You Trust in God's Strength for Your New Marital Duties?

He gives strength to the weary
and increases the power of the weak.

Isaiah 40:29

For what the law was powerless to do in that it was weakened by the sinful nature, God did by sending

78

his own Son.

Romans 8:3a

In the same way, the Spirit helps us in our weakness. We do not know what we ought to pray for, but the Spirit himself intercedes for us with groans that words cannot express.

Romans 8:26

That is why, for Christ's sake, I delight in weaknesses, in insults, in hardships, in persecutions, in difficulties. For when I am weak, then I am strong.

II Corinthians 12:10

For to be sure, he was crucified in weakness, yet he lives by God's power. Likewise, we are weak in him, yet by God's power we will live with him to serve you.

II Corinthians 13:4

We are glad whenever we are weak but you are strong; and our prayer is for your perfection.

II Corinthians 13:9

Can You Delight in the Children God May Send?

This is what the LORD says: "I will return to Zion and dwell in Jerusalem. Then Jerusalem will be called the City of Truth, and the mountain of the LORD Almighty will be called the Holy Mountain."

This is what the LORD Almighty says: "Once again men and women of ripe old age will sit in the streets of Jerusalem, each with cane in hand because of his age. The city streets will be filled with boys and girls playing there."

Zechariah 8:3-5

And Mary said: "My soul glorifies the Lord
and my spirit rejoices in God my Savior,
for he has been mindful of the humble state of his servant.
From now on all generations will call me blessed,
for the Mighty One has done great things for me—
holy is his name.
His mercy extends to those who fear him,
from generation to generation.
He has performed mighty deeds with his arm;
he has scattered those who are proud in their inmost thoughts.
He has brought down rulers from their thrones
but has lifted up the humble.
He has filled the hungry with good things
but has sent the rich away empty.
He has helped his servant Israel,
remembering to be merciful
to Abraham and his descendants forever,

even as he said to our fathers."

Mary stayed with Elizabeth for about three months and then returned home.

Luke 1:46-56

After six days Jesus took with him Peter, James and John the brother of James, and led them up a high mountain by themselves. There he was transfigured before them. His face shone like the sun, and his clothes became as white as the light. Just then there appeared before them Moses and Elijah, talking with Jesus.

Peter said to Jesus, "Lord, it is good for us to be here. If you wish, I will put up three shelters—one for you, one for Moses and one for Elijah."

While he was still speaking, a bright cloud enveloped them, and a voice from the cloud said, "This is my Son, whom I love; with him I am well pleased. Listen to him!"

Matthew 17:1-5

And Jesus grew in wisdom and stature, and in favor with God and men.

Luke 2:52

• You, Too, Are a Child!

How great is the love the Father has lavished on us, that we should be called children of God! And that is

81

what we are! The reason the world does not know us is that it did not know him.

Dear friends, now we are children of God, and what we will be has not yet been made known. But we know that when he appears, we shall be like him, for we shall see him as he is. Everyone who has this hope in him purifies himself, just as he is pure.

I John 3:1-3

"For in him we live and move and have our being." As some of your own poets have said, "We are his offspring."

Acts 17:28

Be imitators of God, therefore, as dearly loved children.

Ephesians 5:1

He chose to give us birth through the word of truth, that we might be a kind of firstfruits of all he created.

James 1:18

Therefore, whoever humbles himself like this child is the greatest in the kingdom of heaven.

Matthew 18:4

Now, O LORD my God, you have made your servant king in place of my father David. But I am only a little child and do not know how to carry out my duties.

I Kings 3:7

He tends his flock like a shepherd:
He gathers the lambs in his arms
and carries them close to his heart;
he gently leads those that have young.

Isaiah 40:11

"Ah, Sovereign LORD," I said, "I do not know how to speak; I am only a child."

But the LORD said to me, "Do not say, 'I am only a child.' You must go to everyone I send you to and say whatever I command you. Do not be afraid of them, for I am with you and will rescue you," declares the LORD.

Jeremiah 1:6-8

In regard to evil be infants, but in your thinking be adults.

I Corinthians 14:20b

FOR PERSONAL PRAYER:

Father, give me the courage to let go of my sin-

gle life, now that you have given me a new life. Transform my hurt about unfulfilled expectations into an openness to receive Your promised peace. Amen

Chapter 5

'Must I leave my parents behind?'

I just can't believe I live two thousand miles away from Mom and Dad!" Florence said, a pained expression on her face. "For the first three months of our marriage Allen and I were living in an apartment right down the street from my old house—the same house where I was born.

"Then my husband got transferred and here we are—half a continent away. I'll only see my folks once a year at Christmas, if I'm lucky. I'm afraid I'm starting to get pretty homesick. And I can tell my sadness concerns Allen, too."

FOR MEMORY:

"I tell you the truth," Jesus said to them, "no one who has left home or wife or brothers or parents or children for the sake of the kingdom of God will fail to receive many times as much in this age and, in the age to come, eternal life."

Luke 18:29, 30

FOR SILENT REFLECTION:

- *Have I ever discussed with my parents how they met and decided to marry? Do I see any similar patterns in my own approach to marriage?*

- *What roles do I expect my parents to play in my new marriage?*

- *To what extent have I determined not to "cut the apron strings"? What are the benefits of this? The unhealthy aspects?*

- *Are my parents dependent on me in unhealthy ways? Have they allowed me to leave home, both physically and emotionally?*

It's Tough to Leave Your Family

The LORD God caused the man to fall into a deep sleep; and while he was sleeping, he took one of the man's ribs and closed up the place with flesh. Then the LORD God made a woman from the rib he had taken out of the man, and he brought her to the man.

The man said, "This is now bone of my bones and flesh of my flesh; she shall be called 'woman,' for she was taken out of man." For this reason a man will leave his father and mother and be united to his wife, and they will become one flesh.

Genesis 2:21-24

"I tell you the truth," Jesus said to them, "no one who has left home or wife or brothers or parents or children for the sake of the kingdom of God will fail to receive many times as much in this age and, in the age to come, eternal life."

Luke 18:29, 30

• *Realize That All Things Come to an End*
There is a time for everything,
and a season for every activity under heaven:
a time to be born and a time to die,
a time to plant and a time to uproot,
a time to kill and a time to heal,

87

a time to tear down and a time to build,
a time to weep and a time to laugh,
a time to mourn and a time to dance,
a time to scatter stones and a time to gather them,
a time to embrace and a time to refrain,
a time to search and a time to give up,
a time to keep and a time to throw away,
a time to tear and a time to mend,
a time to be silent and a time to speak,
a time to love and a time to hate,
a time for war and a time for peace.

Ecclesiastes 3:1-8

•*Turn Your Grief into Giving*

There will always be poor people in the land. Therefore I command you to be openhanded toward your brothers and toward the poor and needy in your land.

Deuteronomy 15:11

Do not withhold good from those who deserve it,
when it is in your power to act.
Do not say to your neighbor,
"Come back later; I'll give it tomorrow"—
when you now have it with you.

Proverbs 3:27, 28

Cast your bread upon the waters,

for after many days you will find it again.

Ecclesiastes 11:1

"Bring the whole tithe into the storehouse,
that there may be food in my house.
Test me in this," says the LORD Almighty,
"and see if I will not throw open
the floodgates of heaven
and pour out so much blessing
that you will not have room enough for it."

Malachi 3:10

Give, and it will be given to you. A good measure, pressed down, shaken together and running over, will be poured into your lap. For with the measure you use, it will be measured to you.

Luke 6:38

For whoever wants to save his life will lose it, but whoever loses his life for me will save it.

Luke 9:24

Therefore, I urge you, brothers, in view of God's mercy, to offer your bodies as living sacrifices, holy and pleasing to God—this is your spiritual act of worship.

Romans 12:1

89

On the first day of every week, each one of you should set aside a sum of money in keeping with his income, saving it up, so that when I come no collections will have to be made.

I Corinthians 16:2

If anyone has material possessions and sees his brother in need but has no pity on him, how can the love of God be in him?

I John 3:17

• *Refocus on Church Life To Make "Letting Go" Easier*

Experience Joy in the Things of God
He will yet fill your mouth with laughter
and your lips with shouts of joy.

Job 8:21

Our mouths were filled with laughter,
our tongues with songs of joy.
Then it was said among the nations,
"The LORD has done great things for them."

Psalm 126:2

Jesus replied: "Love the Lord your God with all your heart and with all your soul and with all your mind."

Matthew 22:37

Blessed are you who hunger now, for you will be satisfied. Blessed are you who weep now, for you will laugh.

Luke 6:21

Finally, brothers, whatever is true, whatever is noble, whatever is right, whatever is pure, whatever is lovely, whatever is admirable—if anything is excellent or praiseworthy—think about such things.

Philippians 4:8

Since, then, you have been raised with Christ, set your hearts on things above, where Christ is seated at the right hand of God. Set your minds on things above, not on earthly things. For you died, and your life is now hidden with Christ in God. When Christ, who is your life, appears, then you also will appear with him in glory.

Colossians 3:1-4

Joyful Celebrating
I will praise you, O LORD, with all my heart;
I will tell of all your wonders.
I will be glad and rejoice in you;
I will sing praise to your name, O Most High.
My enemies turn back;
they stumble and perish before you.
For you have upheld my right and my cause;

91

you have sat on your throne, judging righteously.
You have rebuked the nations and destroyed the
wicked;
you have blotted out their name for ever and ever.

Psalm 9:1-5

Shout with joy to God, all the earth!
Sing the glory of his name;
make his praise glorious!
Say to God, "How awesome are your deeds!
So great is your power that your enemies cringe
before you.
All the earth bows down to you; they sing praise to
you,
they sing praise to your name."

Psalm 66:1-4

Come, let us sing for joy to the LORD;
let us shout aloud to the Rock of our salvation.
Let us come before him with thanksgiving
and extol him with music and song.
For the LORD is the great God,
the great King above all gods.
In his hand are the depths of the earth,
and the mountain peaks belong to him.
The sea is his, for he made it,
and his hands formed the dry land.
Come, let us bow down in worship,

let us kneel before the LORD our Maker;
for he is our God and we are the people of his pasture,
the flock under his care.

Psalm 95:1-7a

Praise the LORD.
Praise God in his sanctuary;
praise him in his mighty heavens.
Praise him for his acts of power;
praise him for his surpassing greatness.
Praise him with the sounding of the trumpet,
praise him with the harp and lyre,
praise him with tambourine and dancing,
praise him with the strings and flute,
praise him with the clash of cymbals,
praise him with resounding cymbals.
Let everything that has breath praise the LORD.
Praise the LORD.

Psalm 150:1-6

Joyful Fellowshiping

Those who accepted his message were baptized, and about three thousand were added to their number that day. They devoted themselves to the apostles' teaching and to the fellowship, to the breaking of bread and to prayer.

Acts 2:41, 42

I thank my God every time I remember you. In all my prayers for all of you, I always pray with joy because of your partnership in the gospel from the first day until now.

Philippians 1:3-5

We proclaim to you what we have seen and heard, so that you also may have fellowship with us. And our fellowship is with the Father and with his Son, Jesus Christ. If we claim to have fellowship with him yet walk in the darkness, we lie and do not live by the truth. But if we walk in the light, as he is in the light, we have fellowship with one another, and the blood of Jesus, his Son, purifies us from all sin.

I John 1:3, 6, 7

Joyful Playing

David and the whole house of Israel were celebrating with all their might before the LORD, with songs and with harps, lyres, tambourines, sistrums and cymbals.

II Samuel 6:5

The hills bring him their produce,
and all the wild animals play nearby.

Job 40:20

This is what the LORD says:
"I will return to Zion and dwell in Jerusalem.

Then Jerusalem will be called the City of Truth,
and the mountain of the LORD Almighty
will be called the Holy Mountain."
This is what the LORD Almighty says:
"Once again men and women of ripe old age
will sit in the streets of Jerusalem,
each with cane in hand because of his age.
The city streets will be filled
with boys and girls playing there."

Zechariah 8:3-5

Feeling Lonely as a Newlywed?

I, the LORD, have called you in righteousness;
I will take hold of your hand.
I will keep you and will make you to be a covenant
for the people and a light for the Gentiles.

Isaiah 42:6

For the LORD will not reject his people;
he will never forsake his inheritance.

Psalm 94:14

"For your Maker is your husband—
the LORD Almighty is his name—
the Holy One of Israel is your Redeemer;
he is called the God of all the earth.
The LORD will call you back

95

as if you were a wife
deserted and distressed in spirit—
a wife who married young,
only to be rejected," says your God.
"For a brief moment I abandoned you,
but with deep compassion I will bring you back.
In a surge of anger I hid my face from you for a
moment,
but with everlasting kindness
I will have compassion on you,"
says the LORD your Redeemer.
"To me this is like the days of Noah,
when I swore that the waters of Noah
would never again cover the earth.
So now I have sworn not to be angry with you,
never to rebuke you again.
Though the mountains be shaken and the hills be
removed,
yet my unfailing love for you
will not be shaken
nor my covenant of peace be removed,"
says the LORD, who has compassion on you.

Isaiah 54:5-10

God has said,
"Never will I leave you;
never will I forsake you."

Hebrews 13:5b

Let In-Laws Help, If They Are Willing

• *Moses: He Learned How to Lead from His Father-in-Law*

The next day Moses took his seat to serve as judge for the people, and they stood around him from morning till evening. When his father-in-law saw all that Moses was doing for the people, he said, "What is this you are doing for the people? Why do you alone sit as judge, while all these people stand around you from morning till evening?"

Moses answered him, "Because the people come to me to seek God's will. Whenever they have a dispute, it is brought to me, and I decide between the parties and inform them of God's decrees and laws."

Moses' father-in-law replied, "What you are doing is not good. You and these people who come to you will only wear yourselves out. The work is too heavy for you; you cannot handle it alone. Listen now to me and I will give you some advice, and may God be with you. You must be the people's representative before God and bring their disputes to him. Teach them the decrees and laws, and show them the way to live and the duties they are to perform. But select capable men from all the people—men who fear God, trustworthy men who hate dishonest gain—and appoint them as officials over thousands, hundreds, fifties and tens. Have them serve as judges for the people at all times, but have them bring every difficult case to you; the simple cases they can decide themselves. That will make your load lighter, because they will share it with you. If you do this and God so commands, you will be able to stand the strain, and all these people will go home satisfied."

Moses listened to his father-in-law and did everything he said.

Exodus 18:13-24

• *Ruth: She Trusted in the Goodwill of Her Mother-in-Law*

In the days when the judges ruled, there was a famine in the land, and a man from Bethlehem in Judah, together with his wife and two sons, went to live for a while in the country of Moab. The man's name was Elimelech, his wife's name Naomi, and the names of his two sons were Mahlon and Kilion. They were Ephrathites from Bethlehem, Judah. And they went to Moab and lived there.

Now Elimelech, Naomi's husband, died, and she was left with her two sons. They married Moabite women, one named Orpah and the other Ruth. . .

But Naomi said, "Return home, my daughters. Why would you come with me? Am I going to have any more sons, who could become your husbands? Return home, my daughters; I am too old to have another husband. Even if I thought there was still hope for me—even if I had a husband tonight and then gave birth to sons—would you wait until they grew up? Would you remain unmarried for them? No, my daughters. It is more bitter for me than for you, because the LORD'S hand has gone out against me!"

At this they wept again. Then Orpah kissed her mother-in-law good-by, but Ruth clung to her.

"Look," said Naomi, "your sister-in-law is going back to her people and her gods. Go back with her."

But Ruth replied, "Don't urge me to leave you or to turn back from you. Where you go I will go, and where you stay I will stay. Your people will be my people and your God my God. Where you die I will die, and there I will be buried. May the LORD deal with me, be it ever so severely, if anything but death separates you and me."

So Boaz took Ruth and she became his wife. Then he went to her, and the LORD enabled her to conceive, and she gave birth to a son. The women said to Naomi: "Praise be to the LORD, who this day has not left you without a kinsman-redeemer. May he become famous throughout Israel! He will renew your life and sustain you in your old age. For your daughter-in-law, who loves you and who is better to you than seven sons, has given him birth."

Then Naomi took the child, laid him in her lap and cared for him.

Ruth 1:1-4, 11-17; 4:13-16

• *Build a Support Network*

How good and pleasant it is
when brothers live together in unity!
It is like precious oil poured on the head. . . .
It is as if the dew of Hermon were falling on Mount
Zion.
For there the LORD bestows his blessing,
even life forevermore.

Psalm 133:1-3

When Job's three friends, Eliphaz the Temanite, Bildad the Shuhite and Zophar the Naamathite, heard about all the troubles that had come upon him, they set out from their homes and met together by agreement to go and sympathize with him and comfort him. When they saw him from a distance, they could hardly recognize him; they began to weep aloud, and they tore their robes and sprinkled dust on their heads. Then they sat on the ground with him for seven days and seven nights. No one said a word to him, because they saw how great his suffering was.

Job 2:11-13

Be devoted to one another in brotherly love. Honor one another above yourselves.

Romans 12:10

Therefore encourage one another and build each

other up, just as in fact you are doing. And we urge you, brothers, warn those who are idle, encourage the timid, help the weak, be patient with everyone.

I Thessalonians 5:11, 14

• *Find Support in Church Fellowship*

Let us not give up meeting together, as some are in the habit of doing, but let us encourage one another—and all the more as you see the Day approaching.

Hebrews 10:25

The body is a unit, though it is made up of many parts; and though all its parts are many, they form one body. So it is with Christ. For we were all baptized by one Spirit into one body—whether Jews or Greeks, slave or free—and we were all given the one Spirit to drink.

Now the body is not made up of one part but of many. If the foot should say, "Because I am not a hand, I do not belong to the body," it would not for that reason cease to be part of the body. And if the ear should say, "Because I am not an eye, I do not belong to the body," it would not for that reason cease to be part of the body. If the whole body were an eye, where would the sense of hearing be? If the whole body were an ear, where would the sense of smell be? But in fact God has arranged the parts in

101

the body, every one of them, just as he wanted them to be. If they were all one part, where would the body be? As it is, there are many parts, but one body.

The eye cannot say to the hand, "I don't need you!" And the head cannot say to the feet, "I don't need you!" On the contrary, those parts of the body that seem to be weaker are indispensable, and the parts that we think are less honorable we treat with special honor. And the parts that are unpresentable are treated with special modesty, while our presentable parts need no special treatment. But God has combined the members of the body and has given greater honor to the parts that lacked it, so that there should be no division in the body, but that its parts should have equal concern for each other. If one part suffers, every part suffers with it; if one part is honored, every part rejoices with it.

I Corinthians 12:12-26

They devoted themselves to the apostles' teaching and to the fellowship, to the breaking of bread and to prayer. Everyone was filled with awe, and many wonders and miraculous signs were done by the apostles. All the believers were together and had everything in common. Selling their possessions and goods, they gave to anyone as he had need. Every day they continued to meet together in the temple courts. They broke bread in their homes and ate together with glad and sincere hearts, praising God and enjoying the favor of all the people. And the Lord added to their number daily those who were being saved.

Acts 2:42-47

There is one body and one Spirit—just as you were called to one hope when you were called—one Lord, one faith, one baptism; one God and Father of all, who is over all and through all and in all.

Ephesians 4:4-6

If anyone says, "I love God," yet hates his brother, he is a liar. For anyone who does not love his brother, whom he has seen, cannot love God, whom he has not seen. And he has given us this command: Whoever loves God must also love his brother.

I John 4:20, 21

• *Support One Another with Your Gifts and Abilities*

There are different kinds of gifts, but the same Spirit. There are different kinds of service, but the same Lord. There are different kinds of working, but the same God works all of them in all men.

Now to each one the manifestation of the Spirit is given for the common good. To one there is given through the Spirit the message of wisdom, to another the message of knowledge by means of the same Spirit, to another faith by the same Spirit, to another gifts of healing by that one Spirit, to another miraculous powers, to another prophecy, to another distinguishing between spirits, to another speaking in different kinds of tongues, and to still another the interpretation of tongues. All these are the work of one and the same Spirit, and he gives them to each one, just as he determines.

I Corinthians 12:4-11

But to each one of us grace has been given as Christ apportioned it.

It was he who gave some to be apostles, some to be prophets, some to be evangelists, and some to be pastors and teachers, to prepare God's people for works of service, so that the body of Christ may be built up until we all reach unity in the faith and in the knowledge of the Son of God and become mature, attaining to the whole measure of the fullness of Christ.

Then we will no longer be infants, tossed back and forth by the waves, and blown here and there by every wind of teaching and by the cunning and craftiness of men in their deceitful scheming. Instead, speaking the truth in love, we will in all things grow up into him who is the Head, that is, Christ. From him the whole body, joined and held together by every supporting ligament, grows and builds itself up in love, as each part does its work.

Ephesians 4:7, 11-16

Above all, love each other deeply, because love covers over a multitude of sins. Offer hospitality to one another without grumbling. Each one should use whatever gift he has received to serve others, faithfully administering God's grace in its various forms. If anyone speaks, he should do it as one speaking the very words of God. If anyone serves, he should do it with the strength God provides, so that in all things God may be praised through Jesus Christ. To him be the glory and the power for ever and ever. Amen.

I Peter 4:8-11

Look to the Future with Hope

"I tell you the truth, you will weep and mourn while the world rejoices. You will grieve, but your grief will turn to joy."

John 16:20

So do not throw away your confidence; it will be richly rewarded. You need to persevere so that when you have done the will of God, you will receive what he has promised. For in just a very little while,

105

"He who is coming will come and will not delay. But my righteous one will live by faith. And if he shrinks back, I will not be pleased with him."

Hebrews 10:35-38

Therefore, since we are surrounded by such a great cloud of witnesses, let us throw off everything that hinders and the sin that so easily entangles, and let us run with perseverance the race marked out for us. Let us fix our eyes on Jesus, the author and perfecter of our faith, who for the joy set before him endured the cross, scorning its shame, and sat down at the right hand of the throne of God.

Hebrews 12:1, 2

If you devote your heart to him
and stretch out your hands to him,
if you put away the sin that is in your hand
and allow no evil to dwell in your tent,
then you will lift up your face without shame;
you will stand firm and without fear.
You will surely forget your trouble,
recalling it only as waters gone by.
Life will be brighter than noonday,
and darkness will become like morning.
You will be secure, because there is hope;
you will look about you and take your rest in safety.
You will lie down, with no one to make you afraid,

and many will court your favor.

Job 11:13-19

For his anger lasts only a moment,
but his favor lasts a lifetime;
weeping may remain for a night,
but rejoicing comes in the morning.

Psalm 30:5

Though he brings grief,
he will show compassion,
so great is his unfailing love.

Lamentations 3:32

FOR PERSONAL PRAYER:

Lord, give me wisdom in my relationship with my parents, now that I have a family of my own. Help me to see how both our households can live in Your love, separate yet mutually supportive. Amen.

CHAPTER 6

'How can we live on this budget?'

When I was growing up, Dad gave me just about anything I wanted, when I wanted it," said Bernadette. "He had made it big in business, and he was about ready to retire when I was still a teenager. I never really thought about money as a thing to conserve. I certainly didn't see it as a potential problem area. In my family, money was just there; always enough.

"Now Rob and I struggle to keep track of every penny. We're too proud to ask our parents for funds, though they do help out occasionally. But we sure could use more of their advice in this area. Things have got to get better."

FOR MEMORY:

Better a meal of vegetables where there is love than a fattened calf with hatred.

Proverbs 15:17

FOR SILENT REFLECTION:

- *What attitude about money have I grown up with?*

- *How have I brought this attitude into my marriage? Has this caused any problems?*

- *How have I experienced God's faithful provision in the past?*

- *What have I learned from those experiences?*

Keep Money's Importance in Perspective

"Do not store up for yourselves treasures on earth, where moth and rust destroy, and where thieves break in and steal. But store up for yourselves treasures in heaven, where moth and rust do not destroy, and where thieves do not break in and steal. For where your treasure is, there your heart will be also.

"The eye is the lamp of the body. If your eyes are good, your whole body will be full of light. But if your eyes are bad, your whole body will be full of darkness. If then the light within you is darkness, how great is that darkness!

"No one can serve two masters. Either he will hate the one and love the other, or he will be devoted to the one and despise the other. You cannot serve both God and Money."

Matthew 6:19-24

"Therefore I tell you, do not worry about your life, what you will eat or drink; or about your body, what you will wear. Is not life more important than food, and the body more important than clothes? Look at the birds of the air; they do not sow or reap or store away in barns, and yet your heavenly Father feeds them. Are you not much more valuable than they? Who of you by worrying can add a single hour to his life?

111

"And why do you worry about clothes? See how the lilies of the field grow. They do not labor or spin. Yet I tell you that not even Solomon in all his splendor was dressed like one of these. If that is how God clothes the grass of the field, which is here today and tomorrow is thrown into the fire, will he not much more clothe you, O you of little faith? So do not worry, saying, 'What shall we eat?' or 'What shall we drink?' or 'What shall we wear?' For the pagans run after all these things, and your heavenly Father knows that you need them.

"But seek first his kingdom and his righteousness, and all these things will be given to you as well. Therefore do not worry about tomorrow, for tomorrow will worry about itself. Each day has enough trouble of its own."

Matthew 6:25-34

And he told them this parable: "The ground of a certain rich man produced a good crop. He thought to himself, 'What shall I do? I have no place to store my crops.'

"Then he said, 'This is what I'll do. I will tear down my barns and build bigger ones, and there I will store all my grain and my goods. And I'll say to myself, "You have plenty of good things laid up for many years. Take life easy; eat, drink and be merry."'

"But God said to him, 'You fool! This very night

your life will be demanded from you. Then who will get what you have prepared for yourself?'

"This is how it will be with anyone who stores up things for himself but is not rich toward God."

Luke 12:16-21

Beware the World's Materialism

You shall not covet your neighbor's house. You shall not covet your neighbor's wife, or his manservant or maidservant, his ox or donkey, or anything that belongs to your neighbor.

Exodus 20:17

Humility and the fear of the LORD
bring wealth and honor and life.

Proverbs 22:4

For riches do not endure forever,
and a crown is not secure for all generations.

Proverbs 27:24

Then he said to them, "Watch out! Be on your guard against all kinds of greed; a man's life does not consist in the abundance of his possessions."

Luke 12:15

Since, then, you have been raised with Christ, set

113

your hearts on things above, where Christ is seated at the right hand of God. Set your minds on things above, not on earthly things. For you died, and your life is now hidden with Christ in God. When Christ, who is your life, appears, then you also will appear with him in glory.

Colossians 3:1-4

But godliness with contentment is great gain. For we brought nothing into the world, and we can take nothing out of it. But if we have food and clothing, we will be content with that. People who want to get rich fall into temptation and a trap and into many foolish and harmful desires that plunge men into ruin and destruction. For the love of money is a root of all kinds of evil. Some people, eager for money, have wandered from the faith and pierced themselves with many griefs. But you, man of God, flee from all this, and pursue righteousness, godliness, faith, love, endurance and gentleness.

I Timothy 6:6-11

The brother in humble circumstances ought to take pride in his high position. But the one who is rich should take pride in his low position, because he will pass away like a wild flower. For the sun rises with scorching heat and withers the plant; its blossom falls and its beauty is destroyed. In the same

114

way, the rich man will fade away even while he goes about his business.

James 1:9-11

When You Fear the Money Crunch . . .

The LORD hears the needy.

Psalm 69:33a

His cloak is the only covering he has for his body. What else will he sleep in? When he cries out to me, I will hear, for I am compassionate.

Exodus 22:27

But those who suffer he delivers in their suffering; he speaks to them in their affliction.

Job 36:15

"Because of the oppression of the weak
and the groaning of the needy,
I will now arise," says the LORD.
"I will protect them from those who malign them."

Psalm 12:5

"Who is like you, O LORD?
You rescue the poor from those too strong for them,
the poor and needy from those who rob them."

Psalm 35:10

115

He will judge your people in righteousness,
your afflicted ones with justice.
The mountains will bring prosperity to the people,
the hills the fruit of righteousness.
He will defend the afflicted among the people
and save the children of the needy;
he will crush the oppressor.
For he will deliver the needy who cry out,
the afflicted who have no one to help.
He will take pity on the weak and the needy
and save the needy from death.

Psalm 72:2-4, 12, 13

For he stands at the right hand of the needy one,
to save his life from those who condemn him.

Psalm 109:31

I will bless her with abundant provisions;
her poor will I satisfy with food.

Psalm 132:15

Do not exploit the poor because they are poor
and do not crush the needy in court,
for the LORD will take up their case
and will plunder those who plunder them.

Proverbs 22:22, 23

The poor and needy search for water,

but there is none; their tongues are parched with
thirst.
But I the LORD will answer them;
I, the God of Israel, will not forsake them.

Isaiah 41:17

Listen, my dear brothers: Has not God chosen those
who are poor in the eyes of the world to be rich in
faith and to inherit the kingdom he promised those
who love him?

James 2:5

•*Trust in God's Provision*
The eternal God is your refuge, and underneath are
the everlasting arms. He will drive out your enemy
before you, saying, "Destroy him!"

Deuteronomy 33:27

If you listen carefully to what he says and do all that
I say, I will be an enemy to your enemies and will
oppose those who oppose you.

Exodus 23:22

Your threshing will continue until grape harvest and
the grape harvest will continue until planting, and
you will eat all the food you want and live in safety
in your land. I will grant peace in the land, and you
will lie down and no one will make you afraid. I will

117

remove savage beasts from the land, and the sword will not pass through your country. You will still be eating last year's harvest when you will have to move it out to make room for the new.

Leviticus 26:5, 6, 10

He will guard the feet of his saints,
but the wicked will be silenced in darkness.
It is not by strength that one prevails.

I Samuel 2:9

Fear the LORD, you his saints,
for those who fear him lack nothing.
The lions may grow weak and hungry,
but those who seek the LORD lack no good thing.

Psalm 34:9, 10

The LORD will keep you from all harm—
he will watch over your life;
the LORD will watch over your coming
and going both now and forevermore.

Psalm 121:7, 8

I was young and now I am old,
yet I have never seen the righteous forsaken
or their children begging bread.

Psalm 37:25

"I tell you the truth," Jesus replied, "no one who has left home or brothers or sisters or mother or father or children or fields for me and the gospel will fail to receive a hundred times as much in this present age (homes, brothers, sisters, mothers, children and fields—and with them, persecutions) and in the age to come, eternal life."

Mark 10:29, 30

"Indeed, the very hairs of your head are all numbered. Don't be afraid; you are worth more than many sparrows."

Luke 12:7

What, then, shall we say in response to this? If God is for us, who can be against us? He who did not spare his own Son, but gave him up for us all—how will he not also, along with him, graciously give us all things? Who will bring any charge against those whom God has chosen? It is God who justifies. Who is he that condemns? Christ Jesus, who died—more than that, who was raised to life—is at the right hand of God and is also interceding for us.

Who shall separate us from the love of Christ? Shall trouble or hardship or persecution or famine or nakedness or danger or sword? As it is written: "For your sake we face death all day long; we are considered as sheep to be slaughtered." No, in all these

119

things we are more than conquerors through him who loved us.

For I am convinced that neither death nor life, neither angels nor demons, neither the present nor the future, nor any powers, neither height nor depth, nor anything else in all creation, will be able to separate us from the love of God that is in Christ Jesus our Lord.

Romans 8:31-39

And God is able to make all grace abound to you, so that in all things at all times, having all that you need, you will abound in every good work.

II Corinthians 9:8

And my God will meet all your needs according to his glorious riches in Christ Jesus.

Philippians 4:19

Cast all your anxiety on him because he cares for you.

I Peter 5:7

• *Use Your Money Wisely*

Honor the LORD with your wealth,
with the firstfruits of all your crops;
then your barns will be filled to overflowing,
and your vats will brim over with new wine.

Proverbs 3:9, 10

Do not wear yourself out to get rich;
have the wisdom to show restraint.
Cast but a glance at riches, and they are gone,
for they will surely sprout wings and fly off to the
sky like an eagle.

Proverbs 23:4, 5

Jesus sat down opposite the place where the offerings were put and watched the crowd putting their money into the temple treasury. Many rich people threw in large amounts. But a poor widow came and put in two very small copper coins, worth only a fraction of a penny.

Calling his disciples to him, Jesus said, "I tell you the truth, this poor widow has put more into the treasury than all the others. They all gave out of their wealth; but she, out of her poverty, put in everything—all she had to live on."

Mark 12:41-44

Jesus told his disciples: "There was a rich man whose manager was accused of wasting his possessions. So he called him in and asked him, 'What is this I hear about you? Give an account of your management, because you cannot be manager any longer.'

"The manager said to himself, 'What shall I do now? My master is taking away my job. I'm not strong enough to dig, and I'm ashamed to beg—I

121

know what I'll do so that, when I lose my job here, people will welcome me into their houses.'

"So he called in each one of his master's debtors. He asked the first, 'How much do you owe my master?' 'Eight hundred gallons of olive oil,' he replied.

"The manager told him, 'Take your bill, sit down quickly, and make it four hundred.'

"Then he asked the second, 'And how much do you owe?'

"'A thousand bushels of wheat,' he replied. "He told him, 'Take your bill and make it eight hundred.'

"The master commended the dishonest manager because he had acted shrewdly.

"For the people of this world are more shrewd in dealing with their own kind than are the people of the light. I tell you, use worldly wealth to gain friends for yourselves, so that when it is gone, you will be welcomed into eternal dwellings.

"Whoever can be trusted with very little can also be trusted with much, and whoever is dishonest with very little will also be dishonest with much. So if you have not been trustworthy in handling worldly wealth, who will trust you with true riches? And if you have not been trustworthy with someone else's property, who will give you property of your own?

"No servant can serve two masters. Either he will hate the one and love the other, or he will be devoted to the one and despise the other. You cannot serve both God and Money."

Luke 16:1-13

So then, men ought to regard us as servants of Christ and as those entrusted with the secret things of God. Now it is required that those who have been given a trust must prove faithful.

I Corinthians 4:1, 2

Be Ready to Help Those Needier Than You

Do not hold back offerings from your granaries or your vats.

Exodus 22:29a

If there is a poor man among your brothers in any of the towns of the land that the LORD your God is giving you, do not be hardhearted or tightfisted toward your poor brother. Rather be openhanded and freely lend him whatever he needs. Give generously to him and do so without a grudging heart; then because of this the LORD your God will bless you in all your work and in everything you put your hand to. There will always be poor people in the land. Therefore I command you to be openhanded toward your brothers and toward the poor and needy in your land.

Deuteronomy 15:7, 8, 10, 11

Blessed is he who has regard for the weak;
the LORD delivers him in times of trouble.

Psalm 41:1

A generous man will himself be blessed,
for he shares his food with the poor.

Proverbs 22:9

"Give to the one who asks you, and do not turn
away from the one who wants to borrow from you."

Matthew 5:42

"So when you give to the needy, do not announce it
with trumpets, as the hypocrites do in the syna-
gogues and on the streets, to be honored by men. I
tell you the truth, they have received their reward in
full. But when you give to the needy, do not let your
left hand know what your right hand is doing, so
that your giving may be in secret. Then your Father,
who sees what is done in secret, will reward you."

Matthew 6:2-4

But just as you excel in everything—in faith, in
speech, in knowledge, in complete earnestness and
in your love for us—see that you also excel in this
grace of giving.

II Corinthians 8:7

Remember this: Whoever sows sparingly will also reap sparingly, and whoever sows generously will also reap generously. Each man should give what he has decided in his heart to give, not reluctantly or under compulsion, for God loves a cheerful giver. And God is able to make all grace abound to you, so that in all things at all times, having all that you need, you will abound in every good work. As it is written: "He has scattered abroad his gifts to the poor; his righteousness endures forever." Now he who supplies seed to the sower and bread for food will also supply and increase your store of seed and will enlarge the harvest of your righteousness. You will be made rich in every way so that you can be generous on every occasion, and through us your generosity will result in thanksgiving to God.

This service that you perform is not only supplying the needs of God's people but is also overflowing in many expressions of thanks to God.

II Corinthians 9:6-12

Command those who are rich in this present world not to be arrogant nor to put their hope in wealth, which is so uncertain, but to put their hope in God, who richly provides us with everything for our enjoyment. Command them to do good, to be rich in good deeds, and to be generous and willing to share. In this way they will lay up treasure for themselves

125

as a firm foundation for the coming age, so that they may take hold of the life that is truly life.

I Timothy 6:17-19

If anyone has material possessions and sees his brother in need but has no pity on him, how can the love of God be in him? Dear children, let us not love with words or tongue but with actions and in truth. This then is how we know that we belong to the truth, and how we set our hearts at rest in his presence.

I John 3:17-19

FOR PERSONAL PRAYER:

Lord, help me to remember that You alone are my ultimate security in life. At the same time, give me the wisdom to handle money wisely, as a means to an end—the advance of Your kingdom. Amen.

CHAPTER 7

'What part will God play in our new family?'

Joseph said, "My parents always took me to church when I was young, and it became a habit for me . . . until I left home. Now it's up to me to decide how I will incorporate into my marriage the spiritual values I was raised to honor.

"I know it means more than just determining to go to worship each Sunday. Somehow biblical values need to permeate our relationship. This will be even more crucial when we take on the responsibility of raising children."

FOR MEMORY:

He will be the sure foundation for your times, a rich store of salvation and wisdom and knowledge; the fear of the LORD is the key to this treasure.

Isaiah 33:6

FOR SILENT REFLECTION:

- *What does "living the spiritual life" mean to you? What does it mean to your spouse?*

- *How much of your spiritual life would you like to keep private, and how much would you like to share with your mate? Have you discussed this together?*

- *To what extent would you say your marriage is based on a biblical foundation?*

- *What adjustments seem necessary in this area? For example, what practical steps could you take to deepen your personal devotional life?*

Build Your New Home on Biblical Principles

By wisdom a house is built,
and through understanding it is established.

Proverbs 24:3

He will be the sure foundation for your times,
a rich store of salvation and wisdom and knowledge;
the fear of the LORD is the key to this treasure.

Isaiah 33:6

"Therefore everyone who hears these words of mine
and puts them into practice is like a wise man who
built his house on the rock. The rain came down, the
streams rose, and the winds blew and beat against
that house; yet it did not fall, because it had its foundation on the rock. But everyone who hears these
words of mine and does not put them into practice is
like a foolish man who built his house on sand. The
rain came down, the streams rose, and the winds
blew and beat against that house, and it fell with a
great crash."

When Jesus had finished saying these things, the
crowds were amazed at his teaching.

Matthew 7:24-28

It has always been my ambition to preach the gospel
where Christ was not known, so that I would not be

building on someone else's foundation.

Romans 15:20

For no one can lay any foundation other than the one already laid, which is Jesus Christ. If any man builds on this foundation using gold, silver, costly stones, wood, hay or straw, his work will be shown for what it is, because the Day will bring it to light. It will be revealed with fire, and the fire will test the quality of each man's work. If what he has built survives, he will receive his reward.

I Corinthians 3:11-14

You also, like living stones, are being built into a spiritual house to be a holy priesthood, offering spiritual sacrifices acceptable to God through Jesus Christ.

I Peter 2:5

•*A Home Where Plans Are Based on Eternal Truths*

And he told them this parable: "The ground of a certain rich man produced a good crop. He thought to himself, 'What shall I do? I have no place to store my crops.'

"Then he said, 'This is what I'll do. I will tear down my barns and build bigger ones, and there I will store all my grain and my goods. And I'll say to

130

myself, "You have plenty of good things laid up for many years. Take life easy; eat, drink and be merry."'

"But God said to him, 'You fool! This very night your life will be demanded from you. Then who will get what you have prepared for yourself?'

"This is how it will be with anyone who stores up things for himself but is not rich toward God."

Luke 12:16-21

"The man who loves his life will lose it, while the man who hates his life in this world will keep it for eternal life."

John 12:25

Do not deceive yourselves. If any one of you thinks he is wise by the standards of this age, he should become a "fool" so that he may become wise. For the wisdom of this world is foolishness in God's sight. As it is written: "He catches the wise in their craftiness."

I Corinthians 3:18, 19

May I never boast except in the cross of our Lord Jesus Christ, through which the world has been crucified to me, and I to the world.

Galatians 6:14

The kingdom of the world has become the kingdom

131

of our Lord and of his Christ, and he will reign for
ever and ever.

Revelation 11:15

Do not be afraid of those who kill the body but cannot kill the soul. Rather, be afraid of the One who
can destroy both soul and body in hell.

Matthew 10:28

"There was a rich man who was dressed in purple
and fine linen and lived in luxury every day. At his
gate was laid a beggar named Lazarus, covered with
sores and longing to eat what fell from the rich
man's table. Even the dogs came and licked his
sores.

"The time came when the beggar died and the
angels carried him to Abraham's side. The rich man
also died and was buried. In hell, where he was in
torment, he looked up and saw Abraham far away,
with Lazarus by his side. So he called to him, 'Father
Abraham, have pity on me and send Lazarus to dip
the tip of his finger in water and cool my tongue,
because I am in agony in this fire.'

"But Abraham replied, 'Son, remember that in
your lifetime you received your good things, while
Lazarus received bad things, but now he is comforted here and you are in agony. And besides all this,
between us and you a great chasm has been fixed,

so that those who want to go from here to you cannot, nor can anyone cross over from there to us.'

"He answered, 'Then I beg you, father, send Lazarus to my father's house, for I have five brothers. Let him warn them, so that they will not also come to this place of torment.'

"Abraham replied, 'They have Moses and the Prophets; let them listen to them.' "'No, father Abraham,' he said, 'but if someone from the dead goes to them, they will repent.'

"He said to him, 'If they do not listen to Moses and the Prophets, they will not be convinced even if someone rises from the dead.'"

Luke 16:19-30

•*A Home with the Bible at Its Center*

All Scripture is God-breathed and is useful for teaching, rebuking, correcting and training in righteousness. So that the man of God may be thoroughly equipped for every good work.

II Timothy 3:16, 17

Do not let this Book of the Law depart from your mouth; meditate on it day and night, so that you may be careful to do everything written in it. Then you will be prosperous and successful.

Joshua 1:8

133

I have hidden your word in my heart
that I might not sin against you.
I delight in your decrees;
I will not neglect your word.
Then I will answer the one who taunts me,
for I trust in your word.
My comfort in my suffering is this:
Your promise preserves my life.

Psalm 119:11, 16, 42, 50

Your word is a lamp to my feet
and a light for my path.
Sustain me according to your promise,
and I will live; do not let my hopes be dashed.
Direct my footsteps according to your word;
let no sin rule over me.
Your promises have been thoroughly tested,
and your servant loves them.
I rise before dawn and cry for help;
I have put my hope in your word.
My eyes stay open through the watches of the night,
that I may meditate on your promises.
Defend my cause and redeem me;
preserve my life according to your promise.

Psalm 119:105, 116, 133, 140, 147, 148, 154

Finally, brothers, whatever is true, whatever is noble,
whatever is right, whatever is pure, whatever is love-

ly, whatever is admirable—if anything is excellent or praiseworthy—think about such things.

Philippians 4:8

For the word of God is living and active. Sharper than any double-edged sword, it penetrates even to dividing soul and spirit, joints and marrow; it judges the thoughts and attitudes of the heart. Nothing in all creation is hidden from God's sight. Everything is uncovered and laid bare before the eyes of him to whom we must give account.

Hebrews 4:12, 13

•*A Home Built on God's Greatness*

He stood, and shook the earth;
he looked, and made the nations tremble.
The ancient mountains crumbled
and the age-old hills collapsed.
His ways are eternal.
I saw the tents of Cushan in distress,
the dwellings of Midian in anguish.
Were you angry with the rivers, O LORD?
Was your wrath against the streams?
Did you rage against the sea
when you rode with your horses
and your victorious chariots?
You uncovered your bow,
you called for many arrows.

You split the earth with rivers;
the mountains saw you and writhed.
Torrents of water swept by;
the deep roared and lifted its waves on high.
Sun and moon stood still in the heavens
at the glint of your flying arrows,
at the lightning of your flashing spear.
In wrath you strode through the earth
and in anger you threshed the nations.
You came out to deliver your people,
to save your anointed one.
You crushed the leader of the land of wickedness,
you stripped him from head to foot.
With his own spear you pierced his head
when his warriors stormed out to scatter us,
gloating as though about to devour the wretched
who were in hiding.
You trampled the sea with your horses,
churning the great waters.

Habakkuk 3:6-15

What, then, shall we say in response to this? If God
is for us, who can be against us?

Romans 8:31

•*A Home Where the Love of God Flows*
So if you faithfully obey the commands I am giving
you today—to love the LORD your God and to serve

him with all your heart and with all your soul—then I will send rain on your land in its season, both autumn and spring rains, so that you may gather in your grain, new wine and oil. I will provide grass in the fields for your cattle, and you will eat and be satisfied.

Deuteronomy 11:13-15

Delight yourself in the LORD
and he will give you the desires of your heart.

Psalm 37:4

The LORD watches over all who love him,
but all the wicked he will destroy.

Psalm 145:20

I love those who love me,
and those who seek me find me.

Proverbs 8:17

"Whoever has my commands and obeys them, he is the one who loves me. He who loves me will be loved by my Father, and I too will love him and show myself to him."

John 14:21

No eye has seen, no ear has heard, no mind has conceived what God has prepared for those who love him.

I Corinthians 2:9

137

Grace to all who love our Lord Jesus Christ with an undying love.

Ephesians 6:24

•*A Home Where Hospitality Reigns*

"I tell you the truth, anyone who gives you a cup of water in my name because you belong to Christ will certainly not lose his reward."

Mark 9:41

"For I was hungry and you gave me something to eat, I was thirsty and you gave me something to drink, I was a stranger and you invited me in, I needed clothes and you clothed me, I was sick and you looked after me, I was in prison and you came to visit me. . . . I tell you the truth, whatever you did for one of the least of these brothers of mine, you did for me."

Matthew 25:35-40

In everything I did, I showed you that by this kind of hard work we must help the weak, remembering the words the Lord Jesus himself said: "It is more blessed to give than to receive."

Acts 20:35

Share with God's people who are in need. Practice hospitality.

Romans 12:13

Suppose a brother or sister is without clothes and daily food. If one of you says to him, "Go, I wish you well; keep warm and well fed," but does nothing about his physical needs, what good is it?

James 2:15, 16

Offer hospitality to one another without grumbling. Each one should use whatever gift he has received to serve others, faithfully administering God's grace in its various forms.

I Peter 4:9, 10

If anyone has material possessions and sees his brother in need but has no pity on him, how can the love of God be in him?

I John 3:17

Entertain strangers, for by so doing some people have entertained angels without knowing it.

Hebrews 13:2

•*A Home of Kind Words and Helping Hands*
Carry each other's burdens, and in this way you will fulfill the law of Christ.

Galatians 6:2

Be completely humble and gentle; be patient, bearing with one another in love. Make every effort to

139

keep the unity of the Spirit through the bond of peace.

Ephesians 4:2, 3

Speaking the truth in love, we will in all things grow up into him who is the Head, that is, Christ. From him the whole body, joined and held together by every supporting ligament, grows and builds itself up in love, as each part does its work.

Ephesians 4:15, 16

Speak to one another with psalms, hymns and spiritual songs. Sing and make music in your heart to the Lord, always giving thanks to God the Father for everything, in the name of our Lord Jesus Christ.

Ephesians 5:19, 20

May the God who gives endurance and encouragement give you a spirit of unity among yourselves as you follow Christ Jesus, so that with one heart and mouth you may glorify the God and Father of our Lord Jesus Christ.

Romans 15:5, 6

•*A Home of Lasting Marital Commitment*
Enjoy life with your wife, whom you love.

Ecclesiastes 9:9a

It is God's will that you should be sanctified: that you should avoid sexual immorality.

I Thessalonians 4:3

Marriage should be honored by all, and the marriage bed kept pure, for God will judge the adulterer and all the sexually immoral.

Hebrews 13:4

To the married I give this command (not I, but the Lord): A wife must not separate from her husband. But if she does, she must remain unmarried or else be reconciled to her husband. And a husband must not divorce his wife.

To the rest I say this (I, not the Lord): If any brother has a wife who is not a believer and she is willing to live with him, he must not divorce her. And if a woman has a husband who is not a believer and he is willing to live with her, she must not divorce him. For the unbelieving husband has been sanctified through his wife, and the unbelieving wife has been sanctified through her believing husband. Otherwise your children would be unclean, but as it is, they are holy.

But if the unbeliever leaves, let him do so. A believing man or woman is not bound in such circumstances; God has called us to live in peace. How do you know, wife, whether you will save your husband? Or, how do you know, husband, whether you will save your wife?

I Corinthians 7:10-16

These are those who did not defile themselves with women, for they kept themselves pure. They follow the Lamb wherever he goes. They were purchased from among men and offered as firstfruits to God and the Lamb.

Revelation 14:4

•*A Home Where We Fellowship with God in Prayer*

This is the confidence we have in approaching God: that if we ask anything according to his will, he hears us.

I John 5:14

Before they call I will answer;
while they are still speaking I will hear.

Jeremiah 65:24

Call to me and I will answer you
and tell you great and unsearchable things you do not know.

Jeremiah 33:3

If any of you lacks wisdom, he should ask God, who

gives generously to all without finding fault, and it
will be given to him.

James 1:5

Then Hannah prayed and said: "My heart rejoices in
the LORD; in the LORD my horn is lifted high. My
mouth boasts over my enemies, for I delight in your
deliverance." And the LORD was gracious to Hannah;
she conceived and gave birth to three sons and two
daughters. Meanwhile, the boy Samuel grew up in
the presence of the LORD.

I Samuel 2:1, 21

If my people, who are called by my name, will humble themselves and pray and seek my face and turn
from their wicked ways, then will I hear from heaven
and will forgive their sin and will heal their land.

II Chronicles 7:14

Yet if you devote your heart to him
and stretch out your hands to him,
if you put away the sin that is in your hand
and allow no evil to dwell in your tent,
then you will lift up your face without shame;
you will stand firm and without fear.
You will surely forget your trouble,
recalling it only as waters gone by.
Life will be brighter than noonday,

143

and darkness will become like morning.
You will be secure, because there is hope;
you will look about you and take your rest in safety.
You will lie down, with no one to make you afraid,
and many will court your favor.

Job 11:13-19

Who among you fears the LORD
and obeys the word of his servant?
Let him who walks in the dark,
who has no light, trust in the name of the LORD
and rely on his God.

Isaiah 50:10

Let us draw near to God with a sincere heart in full
assurance of faith, having our hearts sprinkled to
cleanse us from a guilty conscience and having our
bodies washed with pure water.

Hebrews 10:22

"Ask and it will be given to you; seek and you will
find; knock and the door will be opened to you. For
everyone who asks receives; he who seeks finds; and
to him who knocks, the door will be opened.

Which of you, if his son asks for bread, will give
him a stone? Or if he asks for a fish, will give him a
snake? If you, then, though you are evil, know how
to give good gifts to your children, how much more

144

will your Father in heaven give good gifts to those who ask him!

Matthew 7:7-11

If you remain in me and my words remain in you, ask whatever you wish, and it will be given you. This is to my Father's glory, that you bear much fruit, showing yourselves to be my disciples.

As the Father has loved me, so have I loved you. Now remain in my love. If you obey my commands, you will remain in my love, just as I have obeyed my Father's commands and remain in his love. I have told you this so that my joy may be in you and that your joy may be complete. My command is this: Love each other as I have loved you. Greater love has no one than this, that he lay down his life for his friends. You are my friends if you do what I command. I no longer call you servants, because a servant does not know his master's business. Instead, I have called you friends, for everything that I learned from my Father I have made known to you. You did not choose me, but I chose you and appointed you to go and bear fruit—fruit that will last. Then the Father will give you whatever you ask in my name.

John 15:7-16

FOR PERSONAL PRAYER:

Lord, so often my priorities lean purely toward my own self-interest. Help me to see that the things You want for me are exactly what I need. Amen.

CHAPTER 9

'What does it really mean for us: 'The two shall become one'?'

Andrea commented: "One thing our culture doesn't teach us: a fulfilling sexual relation ship takes time and practice. It's something that a couple learns and perfects over the years; it certainly isn't perfected on the honeymoon! That's why sex would be so unfulfilling outside of a committed marital relationship.

"Of course, the spirituality of sexuality is completely ignored in our media today, as saturated as it is with sexual innuendo. So my husband and I are interested in knowing more about what the Bible has to say on the subject."

FOR MEMORY:

The wife's body does not belong to her alone but also to her husband. In the same way, the husband's body does not belong to him alone but also to his wife. Do not deprive each other except by mutual consent and for a time, so that you may devote yourselves to prayer.

I Corinthians 7:4, 5a

FOR SILENT REFLECTION:

- *What were the attitudes in my family of origin about sex?*

- *How have those attitudes from my past affected my sexuality in marriage?*

- *How well do I communicate with my spouse about my sexual needs and desires?*

- *In what ways does the sexual experience teach me about the nature of God and his view of human beings?*

Rejoice in God's Gift of Sexuality

For this reason a man will leave his father and mother and be united to his wife, and they will become one flesh. The man and his wife were both naked, and they felt no shame.

Genesis 2:24, 25

•*Appreciate Each Other's Bodies*

How beautiful you are, my darling!
Oh, how beautiful! Your eyes behind your veil are doves.
Your hair is like a flock of goats descending from Mount Gilead.
Your teeth are like a flock of sheep just shorn,
coming up from the washing. Each has its twin; not one of them is alone.
Your lips are like a scarlet ribbon; your mouth is lovely.
Your temples behind your veil are like the halves of a pomegranate.
Your neck is like the tower of David, built with elegance;
on it hang a thousand shields, all of them shields of warriors.
Your two breasts are like two fawns,
like twin fawns of a gazelle that browse among the lilies.

149

Until the day breaks and the shadows flee,
I will go to the mountain of myrrh and to the hill of
incense.
All beautiful you are, my darling; there is no flaw in
you.

Song of Songs 4:1-7

My lover is radiant and ruddy,
outstanding among ten thousand.
His head is purest gold;
his hair is wavy and black as a raven.
His eyes are like doves by the water streams,
washed in milk, mounted like jewels.
His cheeks are like beds of spice yielding perfume.
His lips are like lilies dripping with myrrh.
His arms are rods of gold set with chrysolite.
His body is like polished ivory decorated with sap-
phires.
His legs are pillars of marble set on bases of pure
gold.
His appearance is like Lebanon, choice as its cedars.
His mouth is sweetness itself; he is altogether lovely.
This is my lover, this my friend, O daughters of
Jerusalem.

Song of Songs 5:10-16

• *Please One Another Physically*

How beautiful you are and how pleasing,

150

O love, with your delights!
Your stature is like that of the palm,
and your breasts like clusters of fruit.
I said, "I will climb the palm tree;
I will take hold of its fruit."
May your breasts be like the clusters of the vine,
the fragrance of your breath like apples,
and your mouth like the best wine.
May the wine go straight to my lover,
flowing gently over lips and teeth.

Song of Songs 7:6-9

I belong to my lover,
and his desire is for me.
Come, my lover, let us go to the countryside,
let us spend the night in the villages.
Let us go early to the vineyards to see if the vines
have budded,
if their blossoms have opened, and if the pomegranates are in bloom—
there I will give you my love.
The mandrakes send out their fragrance,
and at our door is every delicacy, both new and old,
that I have stored up for you, my lover.
If only you were to me like a brother,
who was nursed at my mother's breasts!
Then, if I found you outside,
I would kiss you, and no one would despise me.

151

I would lead you and bring you to my mother's
house—
she who has taught me.
I would give you spiced wine to drink,
the nectar of my pomegranates.
His left arm is under my head and his right arm
embraces me.
Daughters of Jerusalem, I charge you:
Do not arouse or awaken love until it so desires.

Song of Songs 7:10—8:4

Honor the Call to Sexual Faithfulness

Flee the evil desires of youth, and pursue righteousness, faith, love and peace, along with those who
call on the Lord out of a pure heart.

II Timothy 2:22

Marriage should be honored by all, and the marriage
bed kept pure, for God will judge the adulterer and
all the sexually immoral.

Hebrews 13:4

Enjoy life with your wife, whom you love,
all the days of this meaningless life
that God has given you under the sun—
all your meaningless days.
For this is your lot in life

and in your toilsome labor under the sun.

Ecclesiastes 9:9

In the same way, count yourselves dead to sin but alive to God in Christ Jesus. Therefore do not let sin reign in your mortal body so that you obey its evil desires. Do not offer the parts of your body to sin, as instruments of wickedness, but rather offer yourselves to God, as those who have been brought from death to life; and offer the parts of your body to him as instruments of righteousness. For sin shall not be your master, because you are not under law, but under grace.

Romans 6:11-14

Dear friends, I urge you, as aliens and strangers in the world, to abstain from sinful desires, which war against your soul.

I Peter 2:11

"Food for the stomach and the stomach for food"— but God will destroy them both. The body is not meant for sexual immorality, but for the Lord, and the Lord for the body. Do you not know that your bodies are members of Christ himself? Shall I then take the members of Christ and unite them with a prostitute? Never!

I Corinthians 6:13, 15

You have heard that it was said, "Do not commit adultery." But I tell you that anyone who looks at a woman lustfully has already committed adultery with her in his heart.

Matthew 5:27, 28

Resist Lustful Temptations

No temptation has seized you except what is common to man. And God is faithful; he will not let you be tempted beyond what you can bear. But when you are tempted, he will also provide a way out so that you can stand up under it.

I Corinthians 10:13

What shall we say, then? Shall we go on sinning so that grace may increase? By no means! We died to sin; how can we live in it any longer? Or don't you know that all of us who were baptized into Christ Jesus were baptized into his death? We were therefore buried with him through baptism into death in order that, just as Christ was raised from the dead through the glory of the Father, we too may live a new life.

If we have been united with him like this in his death, we will certainly also be united with him in his resurrection. For we know that our old self was crucified with him so that the body of sin might be done away with, that we should no longer be slaves to sin—because anyone who has died has been freed from sin. In the same way, count yourselves dead to sin but alive to God in Christ Jesus. Therefore do not let sin reign in your mortal body so that you obey its evil desires.

Romans 6:1-7, 11, 12

But the Lord is faithful, and he will strengthen and protect you from the evil one.

II Thessalonians 3:3

Be self-controlled and alert. Your enemy the devil prowls around like a roaring lion looking for someone to devour. Resist him, standing firm in the faith, because you know that your brothers throughout the world are undergoing the same kind of sufferings.

And the God of all grace, who called you to his eternal glory in Christ, after you have suffered a little while, will himself restore you and make you strong, firm and steadfast.

I Peter 5:8-10

Finally, be strong in the Lord and in his mighty power. Put on the full armor of God so that you can take your stand against the devil's schemes. For our struggle is not against flesh and blood, but against the rulers, against the authorities, against the powers of this dark world and against the spiritual forces of evil in the heavenly realms. Therefore put on the full armor of God, so that when the day of evil comes, you may be able to stand your ground, and after you have done everything, to stand. Stand firm then, with the belt of truth buckled around your waist, with the breastplate of righteousness in place, and with your feet fitted with the readiness that comes from the gospel of peace. In addition to all this, take up the shield of faith, with which you can extinguish all the flaming arrows of the evil one. Take the helmet of salvation and the sword of the Spirit, which is the word of God. And pray in the Spirit on all occasions with all kinds of prayers and requests. With this in mind, be alert and always keep on praying for all the saints.

Ephesians 6:10-18

Shun Sexual Promiscuity

"You have heard that it was said, 'Do not commit adultery.' But I tell you that anyone who looks at a woman lustfully has already committed adultery with her in his heart."

Matthew 5:27, 28

For the lips of an adulteress drip honey,
and her speech is smoother than oil;

but in the end she is bitter as gall,
sharp as a double-edged sword.
Her feet go down to death;
her steps lead straight to the grave.
She gives no thought to the way of life;
her paths are crooked, but she knows it not.
Now then, my sons, listen to me;
do not turn aside from what I say.
Keep to a path far from her,
do not go near the door of her house,
lest you give your best strength to others
and your years to one who is cruel,
lest strangers feast on your wealth
and your toil enrich another man's house.
At the end of your life you will groan,
when your flesh and body are spent.
You will say, "How I hated discipline!
How my heart spurned correction!
I would not obey my teachers or listen to my instructors.
I have come to the brink of utter ruin
in the midst of the whole assembly."
Drink water from your own cistern,
running water from your own well.
Should your springs overflow in the streets,
your streams of water in the public squares?
Let them be yours alone,
never to be shared with strangers.

May your fountain be blessed,
and may you rejoice in the wife of your youth.
A loving doe, a graceful deer—
may her breasts satisfy you always,
may you ever be captivated by her love.
Why be captivated, my son, by an adulteress?
Why embrace the bosom of another man's wife?
For a man's ways are in full view of the LORD,
and he examines all his paths.
The evil deeds of a wicked man ensnare him;
the cords of his sin hold him fast.
He will die for lack of discipline,
led astray by his own great folly.

Proverbs 5:3-23

Three People Who Misused the Gift of Intimacy

• *Potiphar's Wife*

After a while his master's wife took notice of Joseph and said, "Come to bed with me!" But he refused. "With me in charge," he told her, "my master does not concern himself with anything in the house; everything he owns he has entrusted to my care. No one is greater in this house than I am. My master has withheld nothing from me except you, because you are his wife. How then could I do such a wicked thing and sin against God?" And though she spoke to Joseph day after day, he refused to go to bed with

158

her or even be with her.

One day he went into the house to attend to his duties, and none of the household servants was inside. She caught him by his cloak and said, "Come to bed with me!" But he left his cloak in her hand and ran out of the house.

When she saw that he had left his cloak in her hand and had run out of the house, she called her household servants. "Look," she said to them, "this Hebrew has been brought to us to make sport of us! He came in here to sleep with me, but I screamed. When he heard me scream for help, he left his cloak beside me and ran out of the house."

She kept his cloak beside her until his master came home. Then she told him this story: "That Hebrew slave you brought us came to me to make sport of me. But as soon as I screamed for help, he left his cloak beside me and ran out of the house."

When his master heard the story his wife told him, saying, "This is how your slave treated me," he burned with anger.

Genesis 39:7-19

• Delilah

On the fourth day, they said to Samson's wife, "Coax your husband into explaining the riddle for us, or we will burn you and your father's household to death. Did you invite us here to rob us?"

159

Then Samson's wife threw herself on him, sobbing, "You hate me! You don't really love me. You've given my people a riddle, but you haven't told me the answer."

"I haven't even explained it to my father or mother," he replied, "so why should I explain it to you?" She cried the whole seven days of the feast. So on the seventh day he finally told her, because she continued to press him. She in turn explained the riddle to her people.

Before sunset on the seventh day the men of the town said to him, "What is sweeter than honey? What is stronger than a lion?" Samson said to them, "If you had not plowed with my heifer, you would not have solved my riddle."

Then the Spirit of the LORD came upon him in power. He went down to Ashkelon, struck down thirty of their men, stripped them of their belongings and gave their clothes to those who had explained the riddle. Burning with anger, he went up to his father's house. And Samson's wife was given to the friend who had attended him at his wedding.

Judges 14:15-20

Later on, at the time of wheat harvest, Samson took a young goat and went to visit his wife. He said, "I'm going to my wife's room." But her father would not let him go in.

"I was so sure you thoroughly hated her," he said, "that I gave her to your friend. Isn't her younger sister more attractive? Take her instead."

Samson said to them, "This time I have a right to get even with the Philistines; I will really harm them."

So he went out and caught three hundred foxes and tied them tail to tail in pairs. He then fastened a torch to every pair of tails, lit the torches and let the foxes loose in the standing grain of the Philistines. He burned up the shocks and standing grain, together with the vineyards and olive groves.

When the Philistines asked, "Who did this?" they were told, "Samson, the Timnite's son-in-law, because his wife was given to his friend." So the Philistines went up and burned her and her father to death.

Judges 15:1-6

• *Amnon*

In the course of time, Amnon son of David fell in love with Tamar, the beautiful sister of Absalom son of David.

Amnon became frustrated to the point of illness on account of his sister Tamar, for she was a virgin, and it seemed impossible for him to do anything to her.

Now Amnon had a friend named Jonadab son of

161

Shimeah, David's brother. Jonadab was a very shrewd man. He asked Amnon, "Why do you, the king's son, look so haggard morning after morning? Won't you tell me?" Amnon said to him, "I'm in love with Tamar, my brother Absalom's sister."

"Go to bed and pretend to be ill," Jonadab said. "When your father comes to see you, say to him, 'I would like my sister Tamar to come and give me something to eat. Let her prepare the food in my sight so I may watch her and then eat it from her hand.'"

So Amnon lay down and pretended to be ill. When the king came to see him, Amnon said to him, "I would like my sister Tamar to come and make some special bread in my sight, so I may eat from her hand."

David sent word to Tamar at the palace: "Go to the house of your brother Amnon and prepare some food for him." So Tamar went to the house of her brother Amnon, who was lying down. She took some dough, kneaded it, made the bread in his sight and baked it. Then she took the pan and served him the bread, but he refused to eat.

"Send everyone out of here," Amnon said. So everyone left him. Then Amnon said to Tamar, "Bring the food here into my bedroom so I may eat from your hand." And Tamar took the bread she had prepared and brought it to her brother Amnon in his bedroom. But when she took it to him to eat, he grabbed her and said, "Come to bed with me, my sister."

"Don't, my brother!" she said to him. "Don't force me. Such a thing should not be done in Israel! Don't do this wicked thing. What about me? Where could I get rid of my disgrace? And what about you? You would be like one of the wicked fools in Israel. Please speak to the king; he will not keep me from being married to you." But he refused to listen to her, and since he was stronger than she, he raped her.

Tamar put ashes on her head and tore the ornamented robe she was wearing. She put her hand on her head and went away, weeping aloud as she went.

Absalom ordered his men, "Listen! When Amnon is in high spirits from drinking wine and I say to you, 'Strike Amnon down,' then kill him. Don't be afraid. Have not I given you this order? Be strong and brave."

So Absalom's men did to Amnon what Absalom had ordered.

II Samuel 13:1-14, 19, 28, 29a

FOR PERSONAL PRAYER:

Thank You, Lord, for the gift of sexuality. Help me always to remember that my desire for sex is normal, healthy, and blessed by You. May this area of my marriage serve to strengthen my love relationship with the special person You have given me. Amen.

The following titles are also available from
Christian Parenting Books:

Bible Wisdom for Fathers
Bible Wisdom for Mothers
Bible Wisdom for New Parents
Bible Wisdom for Parents
Bible Wisdom for Single Parents

BIBLE WISDOM FOR FATHERS

'What if I never had a good and loving father as a role model?'

'How can I build our home on a solid foundation of spiritual truth?'

'How can I handle my frustrations with the challenge of parenting?'

The expectations of a father have never been greater nor a father's role more important. But balancing the needs of marriage and children with the ever-increasing demands of a career often results in considerable stress. How does a father find balance and perspective?

Bible Wisdom for Fathers offers principles employed by successful fathers for generations—given by a heavenly Father who wants to help you be the best dad you can be.

BIBLE WISDOM FOR MOTHERS

'Where can I turn for the courage and
energy I need to be a good mom?'

'What if I've already made many mistakes parenting my kids?'

'How can I raise my child's self-esteem?'

The old saying "a mother's work is never done"
has never seemed more true. Meeting the children's needs while managing a household or
career can be overwhelming.

Bible Wisdom for Mothers helps to answer the
questions often asked by caring, concerned
moms by looking directly at the timeless wisdom of the Bible.

BIBLE WISDOM FOR NEW PARENTS

'How can we manage our own lives, handle the basics of child-rearing, and and still prepare our child for the future?'

'Where can we find help when we feel frustrated or inadequate?'

In today's world, new parents face an incredible challenge. Juggling the demands of everyday home life and careers can lead to feelings of frustration, anxiety and guilt.

In *Bible Wisdom for New Parents*, you and your spouse will discover answers to your deepest concerns—and guidance that has stood the test of time. You will find a God who understands the pains and pleasures of parenthood and can help you face your new responsibilities with confidence.

BIBLE WISDOM FOR PARENTS

'What lasting values can we pass on to our children?'

'How can we cope when we feel frustrated with our parenting responsibilities?'

'How might we best love our kids and do what's best for them?'

Raising kids in today's fast-paced, stress-filled world is an awesome responsibility. And just when you're getting a handle on it, everything seems to change—a child's needs, society's values, the demands of your own life.

In *Bible Wisdom for Parents*, you'll discover words of encouragement, comfort, strength, and love that have satisfied successful parents for centuries.

BIBLE WISDOM FOR SINGLE PARENTS

'What steps can I take to raise my children in the best way possible?'

'How can I cope when I'm feeling lonely?'

'How can I focus on God's goodness rather than on my own problems?'

Raising kids can be a daunting challenge when you have to do it alone. With little or no help, single parents must meet their children's needs and manage a career at the same time.

Bible Wisdom for Single Parents offers time-tested truths that have encouraged and strengthened many single parents. You can find in its pages a heavenly Father who wants to meet your needs and help you lovingly raise your kids.